AF444032

PREFACE

I spent fully one-third of my life in church, never asking questions. I blindly and willingly accepted all that was offered to me every week. My assumption was that my pastor attended seminary, and was thus well-versed and studied in the things he was teaching me. It seemed a fair assumption. Additionally, this man was on salary…it was his job to study the scriptures *for* me, and do nothing *but* that in preparation to feed me the information from scripture that I needed to know. Again, another fair assumption.

Then one day it all ran afoul. I saw something that confused me, and I asked a question. A question he could not answer. I was perplexed. He was supposed to know the answers to my scriptural questions. My salvation, essentially, was in this man's hands. Now, I know some of you are saying "our salvation lies in no man's hands", but I respectfully disagree. Our salvation does indeed lie in the pastor's hands…if we give it to him. It was the incident recounted above that made me realize that. If he didn't know the answer to an important scriptural question, how could I be sure he was leading me down the path to salvation? That's his job, right? His entire purpose is to tend to my spiritual well-being and lead me down the path that results in my salvation. My eternal condemnation or justification lay solely in his understanding of scripture and how it pertained to me.

With this realization came another realization: I had to ask more questions. So I did…and was completely disappointed in the results. More non-answers. Worse yet, the few answers that were offered were obviously contrived, and in no way lined up with the bible I held in my hand. So that was that, and it was time to start seeking answers for myself. The answers did indeed come, and were much more satisfactory than the pastor's answers…because they were to be found within the pages of scripture itself. Better yet, many of the scriptural answers were backed by a non-religious, theologically un-biased second witness: historical documents. I can't even begin to convey to you the gratification that came with answered questions. Especially considering the source of the answers. Knowing that the scriptures of the bible, the very text my entire belief structure is based upon, could indeed answer all of my questions was…well, it was liberating. Not to mention *comforting*. This text could answer my questions without the worry of dogmatic slant or personal beliefs interfering. Before you take offense to that remark, let me remind you of how many priests have recently been exposed as child-molesters. How many Pastors have been caught in adultery with their secretaries? How many have been caught with their hand in the offering plate? I know of one such adulterous scandal here locally, and another (also local) far worse. A youth pastor arrested and convicted for soliciting male prostitution (he was a male himself), and then being restored to his duties as a youth pastor.

Umm, no. That's not okay. Not by any dogma, doctrine or stretch of the imagination. If you've read any of the articles about these travesties, you know the congregational response is *always*: "I just can't believe it! I never saw it coming! Reverend LoveJoy was the nicest, sweetest man I've ever known…"

Don't get me wrong, I'm not saying all pastors, priests and clergy are bad folks, I'm just saying that humans are fallible…to a much greater extent than many of us care to accept. Scripture, the Divine Word of the Father, is *not* fallible.

The main thrust of this work is to encourage you to take your salvation into your own hands, so to speak. Scripture implores us…almost *begs* us…to simply read it. Scripture tells us that it is the *only* knowledge leading to and resulting in salvation. My Pastor proved to me that he did not know the scriptures, the one and only thing given to us that teaches us the intricacies of our salvation. Thus, I had to look elsewhere.

When I began to look to other sources for study, and more importantly, to scripture itself, it created an absolute avalanche of information. I was swamped with facts and scriptures. Of the many things that stood out to me, one rose above all else: it never occurred to me that the bible was written in Hebrew. This was an eye-opener to me. I mean, discovering that the roots of my beliefs lay in Israel, in the Hebrew culture, changed so many things. It opens so much up to understanding…a fuller, *deeper* understanding. If you strip the culture out of any work, you essentially lose sight of all its context. Keeping Messiah and the early believers situated firmly in their true setting, ancient Israel, makes many of the seemingly impossible to understand issues in scripture wholly understandable.

There was one very important issue of interest that came with the understanding that our Messiah and our Creator's chosen people and homeland is Israel. That was the realization that those early Israelites did not have Greek/Latin names like "Jesus", "Christ", "Lord" and "God". "Jesus" as we know Him, is very clearly outlined in the scriptures as being a Jew. A small amount of research quickly resulted in His true, given Hebrew name. When the messenger told Joseph what to name this yet unborn child, the name he was commanded to bestow was "Yeshua". The Hebrew word Yeshua means "salvation". This really demonstrates the significance of our Messiah's true name. Just think of that every time you see the word "Jesus" in your bible: salvation. Your Messiah, the one who was sent to *save* you... His name is actually *salvation*. Research also provided one other note of interest on this subject: the word "Jesus", has absolutely no meaning in Latin or Greek. It is, quite literally, meaningless. This same situation extends to "lord" and "God". Our Creator has a true, proper name just as Messiah does. He revealed this name to His chosen people, Israel. The name is just four letters... YHWH. Also, the term "god" is not to be found anywhere in the original Hebrew manuscripts. The word that acts as His title, as found in the ancient manuscripts, is "Elohiym". So, the true names are Messiah Yeshua and YHWH your Elohiym.

Many argue this, but it is inarguable. This is simply a textual fact. If you don't believe me, look it up. Now, I'm not talking about religious zealots and cultist here... I'm talking about biblical scholars. You may refer to our Creator and Messiah in any way that you wish, for that is not my business, but as for me, and for the purpose of this book, I will be referring to them by their proper names. After all, keep in mind that there is nobody above our Creator... as in, nobody *named* Him. He named *Himself*. If that's what He wants to be known as, then by golly that's good enough for me. The same goes for Yeshua... the Father Himself named Him, so it seems reasonable that He wanted Him to be known by that name. Scripture itself indicates that His name is very important (Acts 4:12). Have you ever seen a scripture that led you to believe our Heavenly Father acts flippantly, or on a whim? I'm positive, with scripture as my witness, that every single thing our Creator does is with reason and good purpose. Now, moving back to the point of this book.

This work is going to follow a basic outline. My intention is to arm you with some *very* important questions to ask your pastor. They are going to address subjects that have everything to do with our salvation. Please note that this is not something I personally *think*, this is something scripture clearly states. You will see this as we progress throughout the book. I will offer you nothing that comes from my feelings, but only that which is clearly stated in scripture, and at that, backed by other scripture and/or historical reference. You see, I don't trust my feelings, because feelings come from the heart:

> Jeremiah 17: [9] *"The **heart is deceitful above all things**,*
> *And desperately wicked;*
> ***Who can know it**?*

> Matthew 15: [19] *For **out of the heart** proceed evil thoughts, murders, adulteries, fornications, thefts, false witness, blasphemies.*

> Mark 7: [21] *For from within, **out of the heart** of men, proceed evil thoughts, adulteries, fornications, murders,* [22] *thefts, covetousness, wickedness, deceit, lewdness, an evil eye, blasphemy, pride, foolishness.* [23] *All these evil things come from within and defile a man."* (emphasis mine)

The issue is that we are fleshly. We are humans, and as such, we are weak. I can assure you, we can justify just about anything we want. Herein lies the problem that we all face: doctrines, dogmas and theologies all stem from the differing viewpoints from within the heart of man. By the end of this book, I promise that I will *prove to you* that this is true. You will see with your own eyes the contradiction between the divinely-inspired Word of the Father, and the mortally-desired words of men. It's a *promise*.

Having spent two-thirds of my life in church, I've had it with dogma and doctrine…I'm only interested in scripturally and historically verifiable facts. Thus, these two things (which seem to be very unpopular these days) are the only things I will present to you in this book.

The basic outline that we're going to follow will be:

#1- The question itself, as the chapter title

#2- The most common and likely pastoral responses

#3- The truth of the matter, as told by scripture

In doing this, you are going to be provided the question, prepared for the pastor's most likely response, and then armed with all the facts and truths of the matter. You will be armed with sub-questions that are extremely important and pertinent to the given subject at hand. Thus, you will be fully and sufficiently scripturally armed to discover the truth about many of the doctrines and traditions we have so blindly followed *and* be well prepared to discuss it with your pastor. As we progress into the book, you will come to see exactly *why* you are going to want to ask your pastor these questions. Allow me to relay a short analogy.

If somebody told you that you had to jump off a cliff in order to save your life, would you do it without question? I'm pretty sure my first response would be "uhhh…why???". I would not risk my life based on the word of any human being on this planet, without first hearing why I should do it, what the point of it is, what the outcome will be and *absolute PROOF* that I should do it.

How is basing our *spiritual* life or death…our *eternity*…on the words of a man any different than hinging our fleshly life or death upon the words of that very same man? If we can agree that scripture does indeed teach that sin results in spiritual death, then I see absolutely no reason whatsoever that we should not be *demanding* absolute and unquestionable *proof* that what we are doing is correct by the Father's scripturally commanded standards.

James 1: "…*¹⁵ Then, when desire has conceived, it gives birth to sin; **<u>and sin</u>**,*

<u>when it is full-grown</u>, <u>brings forth death</u>."

v

1
WHAT IS SIN?

The most likely responses are:

"Sin is anything you are not supposed to do or think."

"Sin is a lot of things."

"Sin is something different for everybody."

The truth:

Sin is much more specific than that. Do you see an issue with the above responses? There was not a single *precise* answer. When asking this questions to pastors, the responses I've received are very ambiguous terms that are defined by absolutely nothing. In addition to not being defined, they are also *backed* by nothing. Scripture does not leave this very important subject hanging in such an abstract, ambiguous way. Scripture does quite the opposite: it defines sin down to the very last letter. Don't get nervous here... though I am going to line this out specifically, just as scripture does...there is nothing to fear. On the contrary, you are most likely going to be quite relieved.

As stated at the end of the last chapter, I think we can all agree that sin is the one thing that will separate us from our Maker for all eternity. As you can see, a pastoral response that does not specifically define sin is quite dangerous; our eternity hangs in the balance. What if you lived your entire life in strict obedience to your denominational doctrine, only to find out on judgment day that your doctrine was in violation of the rules the Creator set-forth? In addition, what if you came to find out that there was no salvation in your ignorance? What if that was because the definition of sin you actually needed to be mindful of was written in black and white, and in the very book you carried to church every Sunday?

It may sound unbelievable, but I assure you that this very thing is true for an enormous number of people. If you will give me a least a few pages, I can prove it to you…with *scripture*.

As previously stated, sin is very specifically defined by the bible. The true answer to this question, "what is sin?", is quite clear when using scripture as our dictionary:

Sin is *lawlessness*:

> 1John 3: *⁴ Whoever commits sin also commits lawlessness, and __sin is lawlessness__.* (emphasis mine)

As I said, very clear, and very to the point. So this now begs a new question: what is lawlessness? Of what law is John speaking?

John speaks of the *only* law ever set forth by our Creator. The only law scripture ever references. The law that He gave through His servant Moses at Sinai. Now, I know this may have just made you do a double-take, but I can also prove with scripture that this is indeed the law John was speaking of. I will do it with Paul's letters, of all things.

> Romans 7: *⁷ What shall we say then? Is the law sin? Certainly not! On the contrary, __I would not have known sin except through the law__. For I would not have known covetousness unless the law had said, "You shall not covet."*
> (emphasis mine)

So we see from Paul's letter to the Roman assembly that this is indeed the law of the covenant delivered at Sinai as evidenced by the reference to coveting. The instruction regarding coveting was issued with the rest of the law at Sinai. Paul does us a great service here, proving that the law being spoken of is the one given through Moses. Paul also goes a step further, acting as a second witness to what John claims sin to be…lawlessness. Paul tells us clearly that the only way to identify sin is to know the Father's laws. Thus, sin is the act of not obeying the law.

I want to add a short, interesting note here. The word "law" is a bit of a mistranslation. The original word for "law" in Hebrew (the original language of the scriptures) is "Torah". By its definition, it simply means to "hit the mark". As in, the Father set a mark for us to attain. The most literal meaning of this Torah is not "law" as we know it, it is simply our loving Creator's *instructions* for a safe and happy life. Most pastors accuse the law of being "heartless" or "legalistic". Let me ask you a question. When you give your child the rule of not talking to strangers, are you imparting something as negative as the connotation of the word "law"? Or are you simply protecting them from dangers they don't yet fully understand? Are you being "heartless" or "legalistic" with your child? Or are you simply protecting them because you love them?

All of that said, the simple fact of the matter is that John and Paul both speak to the extent that disobedience to Torah, our Father's "law", is what actually constitutes sin.

See what I mean about the relief? Sin is not a wispy, changing, relative term at all…it's written down in black and white and there for us to read. No more middle-man, no more interpretations. Just clear, plain, simple instructions. No need to be concerned any longer about where you stand with the Father, the Being that holds your ultimate eternity in His hands…you can now be certain, by simply reading His will for us for yourself. Is that not a load off your mind? It sure was mine. I spent most of my life with a burden of guilt hanging over my head for sins I *thought* I *may* have committed.

We certainly need a few more witnesses that the law is yet required of us. A subject this touchy and polarizing requires a lot of scriptural backing.

Luke 10: *25 And behold, a certain lawyer stood up and tested Him, saying, "Teacher, **what shall I do to inherit eternal life**?"*

*26 He said to him, "**What is written in the law**? What is your reading of it?"*

27 So he answered and said, " 'You shall love YHWH your Elohiym with all your heart, with all your soul, with all your strength, and with all your mind,' and 'your neighbor as yourself.'"

*28 And He said to him, "You have answered rightly; **do this and you will live**."*

So we see here a very clear teaching from Messiah. The Lawyer wanted to know what must be done to inherit eternal life, and Messiah answered with a question. "What does the Torah say?" Essentially, it was a rhetorical question. The lawyer answered with a short-list of commandments, and

Yeshua responded *"Do that"*. So Yeshua clearly, inarguably and irrefutably just said "Keep Torah and you will see eternal life". Let's look at a second, more *specific* witness to Yeshua's teaching of Torah:

> Mark 10: *[17] Now as He was going out on the road, one came running, knelt before Him, and asked Him, "Good Teacher, what shall I do that I may inherit eternal life?"*
>
> *[18] So Yeshua said to him, "Why do you call Me good? No one is good but One, that is, Elohiym. [19] **You know the commandments**: 'Do not commit adultery,' 'Do not murder,' 'Do not steal,' 'Do not bear false witness,' 'Do not defraud,' 'Honor your father and your mother.'"*

This is essentially the same situation, but Yeshua, instead of answering the question with a question, answers specifically with a list of commandments. Notice how Yeshua says "you know the commandments", implying that the man knew *all* of the commandments, not just the ones listed. It has been errantly taught and understood that Yeshua merely reiterated the ten commandments. This is not so…the instruction against defrauding is not found within the ten commandments. It is a commandment found elsewhere in the Torah.

John understood the reality of this, that Torah *abides forever*, long after Messiah's crucifixion *supposedly* annulled the Torah:

> 1John 2: *[3] Now **by this we know that we know Him, if we keep His commandments**. [4] He who says, "I know Him," and **does not keep His commandments, is a liar, and the truth is not in him**. [5] But whoever keeps His word, truly the love of Elohiym is perfected in him. By this we know that we are in Him. [6] He who says he abides in Him ought himself also to walk just as He walked. [7] Brethren, **I write no new commandment to you**, but an **old commandment which you have had from the beginning**. The **old commandment is the word which you heard from the beginning**.* (emphasis mine)

John clearly stands witness to keeping Torah. He is not writing any new commandment to us, but an old one…the one from the beginning. Let's take a quick look at what Paul had to say about keeping Torah:

> Romans 3: *[31] Do we then make void Torah through faith? Certainly not! On the contrary, **we establish Torah**.*

(emphasis mine)

Romans 7: ²² *For **I delight in the Torah of Elohiym** according to the inward man.* (emphasis mine)

Romans 2: ¹² ***For as many as have sinned without Torah will also perish without Torah**, and as many as have sinned in the Torah will be judged by the Torah* ¹³ ***(for not the hearers of Torah are just in the sight of Elohiym, but the doers of Torah will be justified**; "* (emphasis mine)

Yes, Paul really just said "We establish the law through our faith, he delights in the law of Elohiym and only those who obey Torah will be just in the sight of Elohiym. We have our three witnesses now to establish the matter. Yeshua, Paul and John all stand witness that obeying Torah is our duty as sons and daughters of Elohiym.

Let me now relate to you a few passages that will impart the gravity of what lawlessness *results* in. This is what happens when we do *not* obey the Father's instructions:

Matthew 7: ²¹ *"Not everyone who says to Me, 'Master, Master,' shall enter the kingdom of heaven, **but he who does the will of My Father in heaven**.* ²² *Many will say to Me in that day, 'Master, Master, have we not prophesied in Your name, cast out demons in Your name, and done many wonders in Your name?' * ²³ *And then I will declare to them, 'I never knew you; **depart from Me, you who practice lawlessness**!'* (emphasis mine)

So, Messiah Himself teaches us that that we can do anything at all that we want "in His name", but if we practice lawlessness, if we are in transgression of Torah, He will not receive us into the Kingdom. That's a scary thought, and in direct contradiction with a great many doctrines out there, so let's have a couple of more witnesses to this fact.

Matthew 23: ²⁸ *Even so you also outwardly appear righteous to men, but inside **you are full of hypocrisy and lawlessness**.* (emphasis mine)

Matthew 24: ¹¹ *Then many false prophets will rise up and deceive many.* ¹² *And **because lawlessness will abound**, the love of many will grow cold.* (emphasis mine)

Matthew 13: ⁴⁰ *Therefore as the tares are gathered and burned in the fire, so* *it will be at the end of this age. [41] The Son of Man will send out His angels, and they will gather out of His kingdom all things **that offend**, and those who **practice lawlessness**, [42] and will **cast them into the furnace of fire**. There will be wailing and gnashing of teeth. [43] Then the righteous will shine forth as the sun in the kingdom of their Father.* (emphasis mine)

There we have three more witnesses that speak very succinctly to the horrible end the lawless will meet. All of these examples are coming straight from our Messiah as well…this alone should alert us to the importance of this matter. According to Messiah, John and Paul: sin is lawlessness, and the law in question is the commandments imparted through Moses at Sinai. Transgression of that law results in eternal separation from our Creator. You see how scripture will tell us exactly what we need to know, if only we will look to it for our answers? If your Pastor claims that there is a "new law" that was instituted by Yeshua, ask him to show you the scripture that speaks to that effect. Don't settle for "I'll get back to you", or "just trust me on this".

I would like for us to notice that, in the excerpt from Matthew 13, Messiah contrasts for us the righteous against the lawless. Since we now know that lawlessness is transgression of the commandments, this defines righteousness for us. Righteousness is the act of being lawful. That is, obeying the Father's law…His Torah. As with all things scriptural, we are again required to have two or three witnesses to establish the matter (Deut. 19:15, Matt. 18:16, 2Cor.13:1, 1Ti. 5:19). I now offer you that second witness as the full scriptural definition of righteousness:

Deuteronomy 6: *[25] Then **it will be righteousness for us**, **if we are careful to observe all these commandments before YHWH our Elohiym, as He has commanded us**.* ' (emphasis mine)

So there we have it, and defined clearly and fully by scripture alone, no less. Righteousness is obedience to the law, sin is disobedience to the law. Allow me to dispel the pastors rebuttal of "that's the old testament, all that talk about law and righteousness and sin", with a *new testament* witness:

1John 2: *[29] If you know that He is righteous, you know that **everyone who practices righteousness is born of Him**.*

1John 3: *[7] Little children, let no one deceive you. **He who practices righteousness is righteous, just as He is righteous**. [8] **He who sins is of the***

<u>devil</u>, *for the devil has sinned from the beginning. For this purpose the Son of Elohiym was manifested, that He might destroy the works of the devil.*
(emphasis mine)

1John 3: [10] *In this the children of Elohiym and the children of the devil are manifest:* **<u>Whoever does not practice righteousness is not of Elohiym</u>**, *nor is he who does not love his brother.*
(emphasis mine)

2Timothy 3: [16] *All Scripture is given by inspiration of Elohiym, and is profitable for teaching, for reproof, for correction, for* **<u>training in righteousness</u>**, [17] *that the man of Elohiym may be complete, thoroughly equipped for every good work.*

For other New Testament witnesses see also Matthew 3:15, 5:6, 5:10, 6:33, Luke 1:75, John 16:8, Romans 6:16-20, 1Timothy 2:22, 1Peter 2:5 and 1Peter 2:21…just to name a few.

We see how clearly scripture will speak, if only we allow it to. When we pull all of these scriptures together, and we can see them fully in their original context…it becomes nearly unbelievable how twisted the truth has become.

It has been said many times that the "old testament law" was a law of vengeance, one in which love, mercy and grace did not abide. This is very likely to come up when you discuss this subject with your pastor. It has for me on numerous occasions. Knowing that this argument will likely arise, I would like to scripturally arm you with the truth of this matter as well.

1John 5: [2] *By this we know that we* **<u>love the children of Elohiym</u>**, *when we* **<u>love Elohiym and keep His commandments</u>**. [3] *For* **<u>this is the love of Elohiym</u>**, *that we* **<u>keep His commandments</u>**. *And His commandments are not burdensome.* (emphasis mine)

2John 1: [5] *And now I plead with you, lady, not as though I wrote a new commandment to you, but that which we have had from the beginning: that we love one another.* [6] **<u>This is love, that we walk according to His commandments</u>**. *This is the commandment, that as you have heard* **<u>from the beginning</u>**, *you should walk in it.* (emphasis mine)

According to John, keeping the commandments (Torah), *is* love. How can that be? Go and study the Torah and you will see for yourself. The command to love your neighbor, the command to provide for the widow and orphan, the command to not cheat in business dealings…the list goes on and on:

Deuteronomy 15: *7 "If there is among you a poor man of your brethren, within any of the gates in your land which YHWH your Elohiym is giving you, you shall not harden your heart nor __shut your hand from your poor brother__, 8 but you shall __open your hand wide to him and willingly lend him sufficient for his need, whatever he needs__.* (emphasis mine)

Leviticus 19: *9 'When you reap the harvest of your land, you shall not wholly reap the corners of your field, nor shall you gather the gleanings of your harvest. 10 And you shall not glean your vineyard, nor shall you gather every grape of your vineyard; you shall leave them for the __poor and the stranger__: I am YHWH your Elohiym.*

11 '__You shall not steal, nor deal falsely, nor lie to one another__. 12 And you shall not swear by My name falsely, nor shall you profane the name of your Elohiym: I am YHWH.

13 '__You shall not cheat your neighbor, nor rob him. The wages of him who is hired shall not remain with you all night until morning. 14 You shall not curse the deaf, nor put a stumbling block before the blind__, but shall fear your Elohiym: I am YHWH.

15 '__You shall do no injustice in judgment__. You shall not be partial to the poor, nor honor the person of the mighty. __In righteousness you shall judge your neighbor. 16 You shall not go about as a talebearer among your people; nor shall you take a stand against the life of your neighbor__: I am YHWH". (emphasis mine)

Deuteronomy 24: *5 "When a man has taken a new wife, he shall not go out to war or be charged with any business; he shall be free at home one year, and __bring happiness to his wife__ whom he has taken.* (emphasis mine)

6 "__No man shall take the lower or the upper millstone in pledge, for he takes one's living in pledge__. (emphasis mine)

14 "You __shall not oppress__ a hired servant __who is poor and needy__, whether one of your brethren or one of the aliens who is in your land within your gates. 15 __Each day you shall give him his wages, and not let the sun go down on it__, for __he is poor and has set his heart on it__; lest he cry out against you to

[17] *"You **shall not pervert justice due the stranger or the fatherless**, **nor take a widow's garment as a pledge**.* (emphasis mine)

Torah teaches how to actively love one another. Notice the word *actively*. This isn't about somehow forcing yourself to have a warm, fuzzy feeling in your heart for somebody you don't care too much for, this is about *acting in love*, even when you don't necessarily *feel* it. That, friends, is your *scriptural definition* of love. Keep all of the commandments, for the commandments are based on love. If you take any issue with this scripturally derived definition, I challenge you to go and find another definition of love anywhere in scripture. You will soon see that this is the one and only definition Elohiym gave to us. That's not to say that we don't all feel that warm, fuzzy love for our family, puppy dogs and kitty cats. Not at all, I'm just saying that it is not what scripture is talking about when it speaks about love. When you go and find those passages about love, please notice how it's always defined. A mention of love is almost always accompanied by a description of it: fidelity, mercy, graciousness, it does no harm, it always does good, etc…all actions, and more importantly, all commandments of the law (Torah).

So there you have it. A full scriptural definition of sin, and just for good measure, the definitions of love and righteousness to boot. Sin is lawlessness, the law is the Torah imparted at Sinai, obedience to Torah results in love and righteousness, and disobedience results in eternal condemnation. These scriptures should give us a solid, basic scriptural knowledge with which to discuss this matter with our spiritual leaders. I know we've been warned not to sin all of our lives, but did anyone ever define sin specifically for us? Fortunately scripture does. Isn't that a relief?

This discussion of sin, and the resulting scriptural definition of lawlessness has led us quite nicely to our next question:

2
WHAT IS THE NEW COVENANT?

The most likely response:

"The new covenant is Jesus living inside your heart."

The truth:

...is nowhere near this assertion. The New Covenant is yet another completely twisted, and wholly disregarded item in scripture. This New Covenant is clearly outlined by scripture itself...through prophecy, Yeshua's very own words and the recount of Pentecost in Acts by Luke. Let's take a look at what our Creator says the New Covenant is...*in His own words*:

Jeremiah 31: *[31]"Behold, days are coming," declares YHWH, "when I will make a **new covenant** with the house of Israel and with the house of Judah,*

[32]not like the covenant which I made with their fathers in the day I took them by the hand to bring them out of the land of Egypt, My covenant which they broke, although I was a husband to them," declares YHWH.

*[33]"**But this is the covenant which I will make with the house of Israel** after those days," declares YHWH, "**I will put My Torah within them and on their heart I will write it**; and I will be their Elohiym, and they shall be My people"* (emphasis mine)

That is your *scriptural* New Covenant. The thing that makes a covenant...well, a covenant, is that it is an *agreement* between two parties. Every covenant has *terms*...the specifications within the covenant of what both parties can expect from each other. Notice the *terms* of the New Covenant: if He puts His *law* on our hearts and minds, then we shall be *His people*. So what does it mean for Him to put His Torah on our hearts and minds? Does it mean we will instinctively know what is right and wrong, according to His Torah? Nope, that's not what it means at all. Fortunately for us, there is another witness to the New Covenant, and it *fully* clarifies what the law being put on our hearts and minds actually entails:

Ezekiel 36: *[25] Then I will sprinkle clean water on you, and you will be clean;*

I will cleanse you from all your filthiness and from all your idols. [26] *Moreover,* ___I will give you a new heart and put a new spirit within you___; *and I will remove the heart of stone from your flesh and give you a heart of flesh.* [27] ___I will put My Spirit within you___ *and* ___cause you to walk in My statutes___, *and you will be careful to* ___observe My ordinances___. (emphasis mine)

That is the *scripturally defined* terms of the New Covenant. Elohiym fully clarifies through Ezekiel what having the Torah written on our heart means:

[27] ___I will put My Spirit within you___ *and* ___cause you to walk in My statutes___, *and you will be careful to* ___observe My ordinances___.

It doesn't get any clearer than that. Your pastor is going to go off on this, so keep in mind...this is the *word of Elohiym Himself.* Straight from the mouth of the prophets. According to our Maker, the New Covenant is His Spirit within us, causing us to keep His precepts and ordinances. So by Elohiym's own words, He will put the desire to adhere to His Torah on our hearts and minds. It's hard to argue with our Creator...and most likely really bad for our health. When the pastor rebuts, no matter the response, be sure to quote this passage in Ezekiel word for word. See how he answers the question "What does 'He will put His Spirit within us and *cause* us to be obedient mean?'" Most likely, the response will be "precepts and ordinances are only part of the law, like 'thou shall not murder', it doesn't mean *all* of His law". Whatever you do, don't let yourself fall for that answer. If that is his response, ask him to provide you with the scriptural reference to where YHWH divided his law up into different categories. That will close the case, because that is nowhere to be found in the bible. Here's another lesson in context. All of those little headings in your bible, the chapters, verse numbers and the commentaries, are *not present* in the original manuscripts. There wasn't even punctuation. So when you see a heading in Leviticus at a chapter break that says "moral laws", "sundry laws", "ceremonial laws" or anything of the like, keep in mind that those little "understanding helpers" do not exist. When the Torah (law) was handed down from Elohiym through Moses to the people, it all came carrying the same weight. Just read Genesis through Deuteronomy and you will see it for yourself.

Fortunately for us, Elohiym adheres to His own Torah, so He graciously provided for us "two or three witnesses" to this New Covenant He promised to make, thus "establishing the matter". I give you the third witness:

Isaiah 59: *[20] "A Redeemer will come to Zion, and __to those who turn from transgression__ in Jacob," declares YHWH. [21] "As for Me, __this is my covenant with them__," says YHWH: "__My Spirit which will be upon you__, and the words I have put in your mouth, shall not depart from your mouth, nor from the mouth of your offspring, nor from the mouth of your offspring's offspring," says YHWH, '__from now and forever__." (emphasis mine)*

This excerpt from Isaiah does a lot for us…it reiterates the same idea from Ezekiel, that being obedient to the Father's instructions is our end of the deal within this covenant. Notice verse twenty says "to those who *turn from transgression*". We discussed in the last question what sin was. It was…*transgression* of the law. So there you go, that is your fully, clearly and *scripturally* defined New Covenant. Now it's very possible that your pastor will come back with something to the effect of:

"That was a covenant for the Israelites…that was *before* the covenant Jesus made with the church."

If he says that, respond with: "What about where it says forever?" I'll let you see how he responds to that on your own. The truth, of course, is that this Covenant is indeed forever, and for *us*. The writer of Hebrews stands witness, because he *quotes* this very same covenant…specifically, the portion from Jeremiah:

Hebrews 8: *[7]For if that first covenant had been faultless, there would have been no occasion sought for a second.*

[8]For finding fault __with them__, He says,
"BEHOLD, DAYS ARE COMING, SAYS YHWH,
WHEN I WILL EFFECT A NEW COVENANT
WITH THE HOUSE OF ISRAEL AND WITH THE HOUSE OF JUDAH;
[9]NOT LIKE THE COVENANT WHICH I MADE WITH THEIR FATHERS
ON THE DAY WHEN I TOOK THEM BY THE HAND
TO LEAD THEM OUT OF THE LAND OF EGYPT;
FOR THEY DID NOT CONTINUE IN MY COVENANT,
AND I DID NOT CARE FOR THEM, SAYS YHWH.
[10]"FOR THIS IS THE COVENANT THAT I WILL MAKE WITH THE HOUSE OF ISRAEL
AFTER THOSE DAYS, SAYS YHWH:

The author of the letter to the Hebrew assembly (most likely Paul), knew for a fact that this covenant prophetically spoken of in Jeremiah, Ezekiel and Isaiah was the same covenant enacted with the sacrifice of Yeshua. Once again, this is a scriptural fact. There is no room for error or postulation.

Additionally, the author of this letter makes a very important observation on this subject. He says "for finding fault *with them* ", Elohiym had to enact the New Covenant. Notice that there was nothing wrong with the *terms* of the original covenant. The text in all of these prove to us the one and only change that took place, thus differentiating the new from the old…was in *us*, and *not* in the terms of the covenant. Let's be fair to Elohiym here, and be real with ourselves. None of the verses just quoted mention anything to the effect that the terms of the covenant had changed. It did not say "for finding fault with the covenant". Was the covenant not something our Creator created? When we say that His covenant has changed, are we not saying He didn't get it right the first time? Think about that. Is it not far more likely that the fault was within *us*? That *we* didn't get it right? Paul certainly thought so.

The truth is that the change, every time mentioned, was within *us*. What was the change He made in us?

²⁷ *I will put My Spirit within you* and *cause you to walk in My statutes, and you will be careful to observe My ordinances*.

Your Pastor will disagree…but it's important to note that he is not disagreeing with you or me. He's disagreeing with the Father. You yourself stand witness. You just read the very same scriptures I did.

This discussion affords us the opportunity to line out something of interest. The bible, as we know it, is divided into two parts: the "old testament" and the "new testament". There are a few things to note about this. The bible itself never once uses either one of these terms. It is very misleading; it sounds as if there is an "old way" and a "new way". Scripture does not teach, adhere to or even hint at such a division. Let's be honest here. Does it not imply that if there is a "new" way, the "old" way is not nearly as important? Scripture teaches no such thing. Let's see what Paul had to say about the "old" way:

> 2Timothy 3: [16] ___All Scripture___ *is given by inspiration of Elohiym, and is profitable for teaching, for reproof, for correction, for* ___training in righteousness___*,* [17] *that the man of Elohiym may be complete, thoroughly equipped for* ___every good work___*.*
> (emphasis mine)

This, in and of itself, gives us a couple of things to look at. First, and to the point at hand, Paul says *"all scripture"* is profitable for a bunch of good stuff. What we miss, simply because context has been stripped away from us, is what that actually means. At the time of the writing of this letter to Timothy, Mark and Luke were very likely the only gospels yet written. So the only thing that those early believers had that would have been called scripture is the "old testament"…the Torah, the prophets and the writings. That's it. Paul wrote letters, that is a fact. He would have never considered his letters of advice to the different assemblies to be scripture. Matthew, Mark, Luke and John are all historical accounts of Messiah's life, and Acts is a historical recount of the Apostles' days after Yeshua's ascension. The words of Yeshua during His time on earth (including the time between His death and ascension), the words spoken to Paul on the road to Damascus and the Revelation to John are the *only* words of Elohiym directly spoken in the "new testament". Notice also how little was spoken to Paul on his way to Damascus…there's really not any earth-shattering Revelation there. Just Paul's own recount of what happened to him.

All that was simply to make a point. The only thing called scripture during the time of the early believers was what we know as the "old testament". According to Paul, it is incredibly important to *everybody*. Everybody would include *us*.

Additionally, there isn't enough space in this book to list every single scripture the apostles quoted that came directly from the "old testament". My suggestion: get a New American Standard Bible as a study bible. It puts direct quotes from the OT in all caps. You will be floored over the sheer number of quotes from the "old testament" by "new testament" authors. There are sections in Paul's letters where it is nearly every other sentence.

In addition to that, we have found many other quotes over the years that the NASB missed. This proves that the "new testament" is wholly based on the "old testament"…so we shouldn't be surprised by this discovery.

I prefer to call the "new testament" and "old testament' by their more proper names. As I said, those terms are not even found in scripture. The OT is known in Hebrew as the Tanakh. The **T**orah, or Law (the Pentateuch), the **N**evi'im, or Prophets, and the **K**etuvim, or Writings (with vowels added, as Hebrew is written with a consonantal script, **TaNaKh**). The new Testament is known as the Brit Chadasha. This is Hebrew for "New Covenant". This is just a more proper, and *much more accurate* way to refer to them. It helps to dispel the man-made construct of an "old way" and a "new way".

Sorry, we got a little side-tracked there. Let's get back to 2Timothy 3. The other thing I want to point out is what Paul says in verse 16: the Tanakh is profitable for *training in righteousness.* Remember that from earlier? All that talk about righteousness? Yes, indeed, the story of scripture is constant, and courses its way throughout the bible. Be righteous, and avoid sin (lawlessness).

Now, to get back to the new covenant. This talk about the Spirit within us might lend itself as some credence to this "Jesus in our hearts" claim. So let's line that out real quick. No, Yeshua does not reside in our hearts, He resides at the right hand of the Father.

Psalm 110: *YHWH said to my Master,*
*"**Sit at My right hand**,*
Till I make Your enemies Your footstool."

Mark 12: *[36] For David himself said by the Holy Spirit: 'YHWH said to my Master,*
*"**Sit at My right hand**,*
Till I make Your enemies Your footstool

Mark 16: *[19] So then, after the Master had spoken to them, He was received up into heaven, and **sat down at the right hand** of Elohiym*

Luke 22: *[69] Hereafter the Son of Man will **sit on the right hand** of the power of Elohiym."*

Acts 7: *[55] But he, being full of the Holy Spirit, gazed into heaven and saw the glory of Elohiym, and Yeshua __standing at the right hand__ of Elohiym,* [56] *and said, "Look! I see the heavens opened and the Son of Man __standing at the right hand of Elohiym__!"*

Romans 8: *Who is he who condemns? It is Messiah who died, and furthermore is also risen, who is even __at the right hand of Elohiym__, who also makes intercession for us.*

So if the Spirit within us is not Yeshua, who is it? It is the Holy Spirit, quite simply another manifestation of the Father. Yeshua has words for us that will clarify this little quandary for us fully.

John 14: [15] *"If you love Me, __keep My commandments__.* [16] *And I will pray to the Father, and __He will give you another Helper__, that He may abide with you forever."* (emphasis mine)

John 14: [26] *__But the Helper__, __the Holy Spirit__, whom __the Father will send in My name__, He will teach you all things, and bring to your remembrance all things that I said to you.* (emphasis mine)

John 15: [26] *"But when __the Helper comes__, whom I shall __send to you from the Father__, the __Spirit of truth who proceeds from the Father__, He will testify of Me."* (emphasis mine)

John 16: [7] *Nevertheless I tell you the truth. It is to your advantage that I go away; for if I do not go away, __the Helper__ will not come to you; __but if I depart, I will send Him to you__.* [8] *And when He has come, __He will convict the world of sin, and of righteousness, and of judgment__.* (emphasis mine)

There you go, a full and thorough explanation of what the Spirit is. The Spirit is the Helper, sent to *help* us….do *what*?

Ezekiel 36: [27] *__I will put My Spirit within you__ and __cause you to walk in My statutes__, and you will be careful to __observe My ordinances__.*

See how it all makes sense, how it all works perfectly together, if *only* we let scripture do the talking? Yeshua personally explains to us what the Father meant when He spoke of this through the prophets.

You are now armed, fully-equipped and prepared to discuss the New Covenant with your Pastor. The New Covenant is nothing more than a graciously given desire to please the Father…to keep His Commandments. Your Pastor will take issue with this, of that I'm certain. So be prepared and make him explain every one of the above quoted scriptures. You may find that you are very surprised with the answers you receive…or lack thereof.

There is something that is often overlooked about this New Covenant that Yeshua ushered in. The Covenant, as prophesied by Jeremiah, Ezekiel, Isaiah and then quoted by Paul, mentions specifically the two parties involved: Elohiym and *Israel*. So, the next question is…

3
WHO IS ISRAEL?

Response:

"We are Israel. The church is Israel."

The truth:

The term "church" does not even exist in scripture. Now, I know you can go pull some scriptures that have the word church in them, but the word it is translated from has a much simpler meaning. A meaning devoid of the implication that the word "church" carries with it. It simply means an "assembly of the Israelites".

Church- Strong's G1577 - *ekklēsia*

> **1)** A gathering of citizens called out from their homes into some   public place, an assembly
>> **a)** An assembly of the people convened at the public place of the council for the purpose of deliberating
>> **b)** *The assembly of the Israelites*

There we go. Clear and simple. You see, the term "church" as we know it, and as it is used today, very much implies an assembly of Gentile believers. I dare say it is more than just an implication, I have been *told* that…many, many times. Something to the effect of: "I'm a Gentile! I don't have to follow the law!" These folks say this as if it were considered a good thing…like they've been liberated or something. We shouldn't be so quick to cast our lot amongst the Gentiles:

Matthew 18: [15] " ***If your brother sins***, go and ***show him his fault*** in private; if he listens to you, you have won your brother. [16] But if he does not listen to you, take one or two more with you, so that BY THE MOUTH OF TWO OR THREE WITNESSES EVERY FACT MAY BE CONFIRMED. [17] If he refuses to listen to them, tell it to the assembly; and ***if he refuses to listen*** even to the assembly, **let him be to you as *a Gentile* and a tax collector.**"

Sooooo…do you still want to be a Gentile? Here we have our Messiah, Yeshua Himself, likening Gentiles to tax-collectors. We know how well tax collectors are loved, right? I mean, don't you just want to invite the IRS right into your home for dinner to look over the last ten years of tax returns?

Yes, I'm aware that Yeshua dined with tax-collectors. But don't forget *why* He dined with tax-collectors:

Matthew 9: *[11] When the Pharisees saw this, they said to His disciples, " Why is your Teacher eating with the __tax collectors__ and sinners?" [12] But when Yeshua heard this, He said, "It is not those who are healthy who need a physician, __but those who are sick__."*

So you see, He dined with the tax-collectors in order to try and turn them from their ways. Therefore, the connection Yeshua made in Matthew 9 between the two is a very negative connotation. The healthy don't need the doctor, the sick do. So Yeshua comparing Gentiles to tax-collectors is a really *bad* thing. You can see clearly within the context of Matthew 18 another contrast: Yeshua is speaking to the Jews. You see, in scripture, Gentiles are anyone *other than* Jews. So Yeshua, by default, shows us that Gentiles are *not* brothers and sisters within the assembly of the Israelites. Stay with me for just a minute. There is a way for Gentiles to be counted amongst the brethren, and we will get to that in just a moment. First we need one more witness to the undesirable standing of Gentiles:

Matthew 15: *[21] Yeshua went away from there, and withdrew into the district of Tyre and Sidon. [22] And a __Canaanite__ woman from that region came out and began to cry out, saying, "Have mercy on me, Master, Son of David; my daughter is cruelly demon-possessed." [23] But He did not answer her a word. And His disciples came and implored Him, saying, "Send her away, because she keeps shouting at us." [24] But He answered and said, "I was sent __only to the lost sheep of the house of Israel__." [25] But she came and began to bow down before Him, saying, "Master, help me!" [26] And He answered and said, "It is not good to take the __children's bread__ and throw it __to the dogs__." [27] But she said, "Yes, Master; but even the __dogs__ feed on the crumbs which fall from their masters' table."*

There are several things to notice here. First and foremost, Yeshua unequivocally states that He came *ONLY* for the lost sheep of the house of *Israel*. The second thing, which is every bit as important as the first, is the *contrast* that *proves* Gentiles have not replaced Israel…He calls Gentiles "dogs". Keep in mind Gentile simply means those from other countries…*any* other country. The Canaanite woman was a gentile by definition. The third thing, and again, just as important as the first two, is the fact that the woman's *fidelity* was rewarded with the granting of her request. Yes, I said fidelity:

"Faith"-Strong's G4102 - *pistis*

1)   the conviction that God exists and is the creator and ruler of all things, the provider and bestower of eternal salvation through Messiah
2)   fidelity, faithfulness

She acted. She did not sit aside and *hope*, she went and sought out Yeshua, and begged for His healing because she knew He was the Messiah. It is beyond important to note the sequence of events here. The gentile *came to* Yeshua, not the other way around. This is clearly outlined in verse 24. What did He say when she arrived? "I'm not here for you, I'm here for Israel".

So His granting of her request…was it because Yeshua was a hypocrite, going against His very own words one sentence before? Or is it because she *proved* that she wanted to be counted amongst the children of Israel? You'll notice she professed that she wished Him to be her Master. Again, very important to note…as is her humility.

We well know that Yeshua is not a hypocrite. So the Canaanite woman must have sufficiently proven her desire to join with Israel. This is what I was talking about when I said there was a way for Gentiles to become a part of the body of Messiah. We have to *renounce* our pagan, Gentile heritage and ways and *take on* the heritage and ways of Israel.

I know this may be a bit hard to swallow, but I can prove that this is how it works. The only way that this can work, all of scripture considered and Messiah's words included, is that Gentiles *become a part* of Israel. We do not *replace* Israel, we *join* Israel. You see, the idea that Israel was replaced by the church is known as "replacement theology", and is an absolute joke. This theology is wholly accepted within most all modern Christian religions, but the simple fact of the matter is this: there is not one single, tangible, *shred* of scriptural evidence to support this theology. On the other hand, there is a *ton* of scriptural evidence for our *inclusion* into Israel. Let's look at that now, starting with Paul:

Ephesians 2: *[11]Therefore remember that formerly you, <u>the Gentiles in the flesh…</u>*

[12]remember that you were at that time separate from Messiah, <u>excluded from the commonwealth of Israel</u>, and <u>strangers to the covenants of promise,</u> having no hope and without Elohiym in the world.

[13]But now in Messiah Yeshua, you <u>who formerly were far off have been brought near</u> by the blood of Messiah.

[19]So then <u>you are no longer strangers and aliens,</u> but you are <u>fellow citizens with the saints,</u> and <u>are of Elohiym's household,</u> (emphasis mine)

That pretty much seals the deal. He reminds them that they were at one time excluded from the commonwealth of…who? Israel. He then reminds them that Messiah's shed blood brought them near…to what? The very thing they were once excluded from: the commonwealth of Israel. That's pretty much a walk-off homerun, but to stay with the theme of two or three witnesses, let's go ahead and look at a few more passages.

Romans 11: *[16]If the first piece of dough is holy, the lump is also; and if <u>the root</u> is holy, <u>the branches</u> are too.*

[17]But if some of the branches were broken off, and you, being a wild olive, <u>were grafted in among them and became partaker with them of the rich root of the olive tree,</u>

[18]do not be arrogant toward the branches; but if you are arrogant, remember that it is not you who supports the root, <u>but the root supports you.</u>

[19]You will say then, <u>"Branches were broken off so that I might be grafted in."</u>

[20]Quite right, they were broken off for their unbelief, but you stand by your faith (gr. pistus-fidelity/faithfulness). *Do not be conceited, but fear;*

[21]for if Elohiym did not spare <u>the natural branches</u>, He will not spare you, either.

²²Behold then the kindness and severity of Elohiym; to those who fell, severity, but to you, Elohiym's kindness, if you continue in His kindness; otherwise you also will be cut off.

*²³And they also, if they do not continue in their unbelief, will be grafted in, for **<u>Elohiym is able to graft them in again</u>**.*

*²⁴For if you were cut off from what is by nature a **<u>wild olive tree</u>**, and were grafted contrary to nature into a **<u>cultivated olive tree</u>**, how much more will these who are the **<u>natural branches be grafted into their own olive tree</u>**?*

*²⁵For I do not want you, brethren, to be uninformed of this mystery--so that you will not be wise in your own estimation--that a partial hardening has happened to Israel **<u>until</u>** the fullness of the Gentiles has come in;*

*²⁶and so **<u>all Israel</u>** will be saved; just as it is written,*
"THE DELIVERER WILL COME FROM ZION,
HE WILL REMOVE UNGODLINESS FROM JACOB."
²⁷"THIS IS MY COVENANT WITH THEM,
WHEN I TAKE AWAY THEIR SINS." (emphasis mine)

There's that grafting in thing. Grafted into what? The cultivated olive tree that is Israel. Paul leaves no room for misunderstanding. He says that the Gentiles have to "come in" to Israel. Couple that with verse 26: "and so *all Israel* will be saved", and our bases are thoroughly covered. Paul not only points out to us twice that it's all about Israel, he does us an incredible service by explaining to us that we must *join* with Israel…not *replace* them. In keeping with our theme of "two or three" witnesses, let's look at one more scripture, this time from the Tanakh, that backs our conclusion:

Isaiah 56: ²"How blessed is the man who does this,
And the son of man who takes hold of it;
***<u>Who keeps from profaning the Sabbath</u>**,*
And keeps his hand from doing any evil."
⁴For thus says YHWH,
***<u>"To the eunuchs who keep My Sabbaths</u>**,*
***<u>and choose what pleases Me</u>**,*
<u>and hold fast My covenant</u>**, ⁵To them **<u>I will give in My house and within My</u>
<u>walls a memorial…</u>"   (emphasis mine)

Here we have our Creator, in His own words, explaining to us that *if* we adhere to *His ways*, and *shun our own*, then He will give to us a memorial and a name with the walls of His Kingdom. It's really a good thing we had the opportunity to line this out. We have here another reference to His "covenant". Something you may have noticed in all these scriptures about the New Covenant, one of its basic criteria, was that it is *only made* with Israel.

Jeremiah 31: *[31]"Behold, days are coming," declares YHWH, "when I will make a __new covenant__ with the __house of Israel__ and with the __house of Judah__,*

So, the truth of the matter concerning this "who is Israel" thing…is that *Israel* is Israel. Always has been, always will be. Israel is compromised of His chosen people. We can be a Jew or we can be a Gentile, it doesn't matter, but as soon as He makes His covenant with us, we become a part of Israel. When He makes His Covenant with us, we become a partaker in all that being a part of Israel entails. This includes the instructions and stipulations for being a part of the commonwealth, just as becoming a naturalized citizen of the United States requires adherence U.S. societal laws. This brings us to our next question:

4
WHY DON'T WE CELEBRATE THE FEASTS?

Response:

"That was a part of the old law"

"That's an old testament law…we're the new testament church"

"Huh?"

The truth:

To start, we just covered the "old/new testament" thing. We have also discussed the "church" thing, and proven *scripturally* that these terms do not exist, they are merely *man-made* false-constructs. The "church" has not replaced Israel. It has tried like the devil, but as scripture has shown, it cannot. Additionally, we scripturally exposed the idea of there being a "new" law. We have discovered that there is no "new" law, only a New Covenant. The "law", as it is called, is merely the terms of that covenant, and the terms have not changed.

You may be unaware of this, as I once was, but our Father instituted a yearly festival cycle of feasts that He commanded us to observe. There's a great example of how "mean and heartless" the "old law" is: a command to get together several times a year and party. Anyway, His feast cycle is highly meaningful and very important. He tells us clearly that when we observe His appointed times, He Himself is there to meet with us. For the purpose of this writing, I am not going to fully cover the festival cycle in detail. I have already done so in another book which I will humbly refer you to at the end of this work. The purpose of this writing is to merely arm you with the basics and hopefully cause you to look deeper into the truth of the scriptures. Therefore, we are just going to cover a few of the more obvious mentions in the Brit Chadasha to stand as witness that Yeshua and His early followers observed these appointed time. I will give you a short overview however, so you can look into these for yourself. The feasts are:

1. Passover
2. Unleavened Bread
3. First Fruits
4. Pentecost
5. Day of Trumpets
6. Day of Atonement
7. Tabernacles

There are plenty of "new testament" reasons to celebrate these feasts. There are many references to them, many examples of them being observed and even an explicit instruction to do so. Let's start with the Feast of Pentecost. We just discussed the New Covenant, so this is a great place to start. The New Covenant was delivered, and fully realized, on the Feast of Pentecost... a scripturally commanded Holy day.

Acts 2: *When the __day of Pentecost__ had come, they were all together in one place. [2] And suddenly there came from heaven a noise like a violent rushing wind, and it filled the whole house where they were sitting. [3] And there appeared to them tongues as of fire distributing themselves, and they rested on each one of them. [4] And they were all filled with the Holy Spirit and began to speak with other tongues, as the Spirit was giving them utterance.*

[5] Now there were Jews living in Jerusalem, devout men from every nation under heaven. [6] And when this sound occurred, the crowd came together, and were bewildered because each one of them was hearing them speak in his own language. [7] They were amazed and astonished, saying, "Why, are not all these who are speaking Galileans? (emphasis mine)

This is something I missed for many, many years. I guess I just assumed the Day of Pentecost was something unimportant. When no one is teaching you the Tanakh, you miss out on stuff like this. The Day of Pentecost is by no means unimportant. Much the opposite, it is *commanded*:

Leviticus 23: *[15]'You shall also count for yourselves from the day after the Sabbath, from the day when you brought in the sheaf of the wave offering; there shall be seven complete Sabbaths.*

[16]'You shall count fifty days to the day after the seventh Sabbath; then you shall present a new grain offering to YHWH.

[21] On this same day you shall make a proclamation as well; you are to have a

As you can see, the Day of Pentecost is a commandment, it is a special Sabbath, and it is to be honored *forever*. There's another question for your pastor: "What does forever mean?"

Something that also flies under the radar on this issue is the obvious: Peter and the Apostles were gathered together celebrating the feast. Also notice that this was after Messiah's crucifixion. If Yeshua's death indeed nullified the "old law" as Christian doctrine teaches, then Peter and the Apostles were hypocrites. They were assembled according to the command we just read in Leviticus 23. Do you think it's even remotely possible that they were not hypocrites, but rather understood the meaning of the word "forever"?

You see, in the church we have totally ignored and discarded this commandment; it has been swept under the rug as a part of the Torah. I do not understand why, as it is the anniversary of the day that the Spirit was sent to us. The very thing that saves us, the very thing Messiah had to be *tortured and crucified* for, occurred on this very day. Everything about our salvation, as taught by scripture, hinges on this impartation of the New Covenant. When we look at the command to celebrate it, and we take into account the perfect purpose of our Creator… it's mind-boggling as to why we have forsaken this commandment. We don't seriously think that this was just a coincidence, do we? That YHWH accidentally allowed something as important as the giving of the New Covenant to just happen to fall on a Holy day He had previously sanctified and commanded? Do you know why the feast of Pentecost was even commanded to begin with? Because it was the anniversary of the giving of the *Old Covenant*.

Pentecost was given as a festival of remembrance of the day the Israelites were given the Torah at Sinai. It goes something like this: Passover was the last day the Israelites were in Egypt. According to Exodus 12:1, the month they were in had just become the first month and Passover was in the middle of it on the fourteenth day. So two weeks after they left, the second month began and after that, of course, came the third month. Exodus 19:1 says that they arrived in the Sinai Desert in the third month on the very day, which means the day the third month began, they camped before the

Mountain. Pentecost commemorates the day they received the Torah and that was on the sixth day of the third month. It's forty-nine days after First Fruits which is the Sunday after Passover. So on the sixth day after they arrived at Mt. Sinai they received the Torah from the mouth of YHWH (Exodus 20:1). This is the original meaning for keeping the feast as a memorial.

So the Old Covenant and the New Covenant were given on the same day, to the same people, with the same terms. For the life of me I can't see any logical reason not to observe this feast. From a *scriptural* perspective…well, it seems to me we had *ought* to, since it was commanded to be observed *forever*.

There is something that this realization entails: if we keep this feast, as scripture clearly commands, then we have to keep the *other* feasts in the feast cycle. Yes, there are seven total feasts, and guess what? They are all just like Pentecost. They are all commanded to be observed *forever*. We absolutely *have* to observe the first three in the cycle (Passover, Unleavened Bread and First Fruits) in order to keep Pentecost. You'll notice the date of Pentecost depends on the date of First Fruits in the command in Leviticus 23. By proxy, First Fruits depends on the dates of Unleavened Bread, which in turn depends on the date of Passover.

If you've made it this far with your pastor, he's most likely about to break out the "Jew-whippin' stick":

"Oh, don't worry about those…those are Jewish feasts".

Wrong. They are feasts commanded to be kept by those who join Elohiym's chosen people, Israel. When he comes back with that response, show him this:

1Corinthians 5: *⁷<u>**Clean out the old leaven**</u> so that you may be a new lump, just as you are in fact <u>**unleavened**</u>. For <u>**Messiah our Passover also has been sacrificed**</u>.*

*⁸Therefore <u>**let us celebrate the feast**</u>, not with <u>**old leaven**</u>, nor with <u>**the leaven**</u> of malice and wickedness, but with <u>**the unleavened bread**</u> of sincerity and truth.* (emphasis mine)

When you go and read Leviticus 23 to learn about these Holy feasts, all the talk of leaven and unleavened will make a ton of sense. For our purposes here, Paul slams the door on the idea of these being feasts that were just for the Jews. You'll notice he speaks of Unleavened Bread and Passover…and then inarguably states *"Therefore let us celebrate the feast"*. Paul understood that the feasts were for Israel. He also understood that if we are a part of the New Covenant, we *are* Israel. Something people do not understand sometimes, is that Israelites and Jews are two separate things. Being one does not make you the other. Just like not all Arabs are Muslim, and not all Christians are Americans. A Jew is one who adheres to the Religion of Judaism. An Israelite is an inhabitant of Israel. In the scriptural sense, any who are of Elohiym's chosen are called Israel, because that's the name He chose to give us. Additionally, upon His return, we will all be inhabitants of the land of Israel (according to scripture).

Now, back to 1 Corinthians. Yes, that's Paul himself teaching us to celebrate Passover and Unleavened Bread. If you are not aware of it yet, Paul and his letters are the entire basis for modern Christian Doctrine. If you are reading this book, then you are most likely a truth-seeker…and this little fact about Paul will become all too clear to you very soon. So why do we revere so much of what Paul said, but in turn discard obvious statements such as this?

The Jew-whippin' stick.

Our pastors have taught us throughout the centuries that the "old, Jewish way" has no bearing on us. Scripture stands opposed to that idea, as well as Paul. We have just seen *scriptural* witnesses and proof that we should observe the festival cycle that our Creator commanded us to keep. He said to do it forever. Again, forever is a very permanent word. We also have other examples of Paul keeping the feasts, as well as Yeshua:

Acts 18: *[19] And he came to Ephesus, and left them there; but he himself entered the synagogue and reasoned with the Jews. [20] When they asked him to stay a longer time with them, he did not consent, [21] but took leave of them, saying, "**I must by all means keep this coming feast in Jerusalem**;"*
(emphasis mine)

John 2: *[13] Now **the Passover** of the Jews was at hand, and **Yeshua went up to Jerusalem**.*   (emphasis mine)

John 7: *[2] Now the Jews' **Feast of Tabernacles** was at hand.*   (emphasis mine)

John 7: *[10] But when His brothers had gone up, then He also **went up to** *__the feast__, not openly, but as it were in secret.* (emphasis mine)

Luke 22: [15] *And He said to them, "I have earnestly desired to **eat this Passover** with you before I suffer;"* (emphasis mine)

We see here Paul hurrying to attend one of the feasts, and Yeshua attending not one, but two Passovers as well as the Feast of Tabernacles (more properly known as Sukkot). So if Yeshua kept the feasts…why don't we? Your pastor may say "Of course Jesus kept the Jewish feasts…He had to live by the law, He was a Jew". Yes, they will acknowledge that little fact. At this point, they've painted themselves into a corner, because we have these verses on our side:

1John 2: [6] **He who says he abides in Him ought himself also to __walk just as He walked__.**

1Corinthians 11: [1] *Imitate me, just as I also **imitate Messiah**.*

Kind of hard to imitate Him, and walk just as He walked, if we don't keep the Torah as He did…wouldn't you say? This is one of the greatest hypocrisies of the pulpit and its teachings. They will acknowledge the fact that Messiah was Jewish and adhered to the Torah, but they stop short of these verses that clearly tell us to live as He lived.

So the question of, "Why do we not keep the feasts?" has not been fully answered yet. We have seen why we *should*, but have not yet discussed why we *do not*. Let me show you why the church does not adhere to the commands. It's because the early church Father's *invented* the Jew-whippin' stick:

From the Council of Laodicea, 364 AD (Catholic council codifying church doctrine):

CANON XXXVII.

IT is not lawful to receive portions sent from the feasts of Jews or heretics, nor to feast together with them.

CANON XXXVIII.

IT is not lawful to receive unleavened bread from the Jews, nor to be partakers of their impiety.

So we see that the early church fathers codified into church *law* that

"Christians" could not keep the feasts that we have proven Messiah, Paul and the Apostles did. Doesn't make much sense, does it? Well, it makes sense when we come to realize the early church fathers were not necessarily well-meaning folks, but rather anti-Semitic. Very, *very* anti-Semitic. You see the proof in the above canons. Calling the unleavened bread of the Jews "impiety", when we have just seen Paul himself instruct us to keep that very feast. Let's take a look at one more. Please be sure to read my note after this selection.

The Constantine Creed:

"I renounce all customs, rites, legalisms, unleavened breads and sacrifices of lambs of the Hebrews, and all the other feasts of the Hebrews, sacrifices, prayers, aspirations, purifications, sanctifications, and propitiations, and fasts and new moons, and Sabbaths, and superstitions, and hymns and chants, and observances and synagogues. absolutely everything Jewish, every Law, rite and custom and if afterwards I shall wish to deny and return to Jewish superstition, or shall be found eating with Jews, or feasting with them, or secretly conversing and condemning the Christian religion instead of openly confuting them and condemning their vain faith, then let the trembling of Cain and the leprosy of Gehazi cleave to me, as well as the legal punishments to which I acknowledge myself liable. And may I be an anathema in the world to come, and may my soul be set down with Satan and the devils."

(Assemani, Stefano Evodio, 1711-1782. Johannis V. Lusitanorum regis e Bibliotheca apostolica vaticana prodeunt. Stephanus Evodius Assemanus ... c Romae: typis J. Collini, 1748)

You can verify this for yourself by looking into the bibliographia of the University of Southern California: http://monasticmatrix.usc.edu/bibliographia.

I want to make a quick author's note here. This creed may be wrongly attributed to Constantine. The earliest date we have for this creed is the date listed: 1748. Constantine died over 1300 years before this publishing. However, it makes no difference if this quote belongs to Constantine or not. It is still a creed that resides within Catholic literature. It is cited as part of the Pope's Library in the Vatican (Bibliotheca Apostolica Vaticana).

So there you have it. The reason we do not celebrate any of the feasts that the early apostles and disciples celebrated. We don't do it because Mother Catholic has forbidden us. Please, keep in mind the absolute authority of the word of the Father. Remember that He said these feasts were to be observed *forever*. His word over rules that of any man, *including* the Pope.

My hope is that you see the lack of scriptural basis for the church's dismissal of the feast days, and the importance of the Divine Word of the Father as reason to go and search out the truth for yourself about the Father's Holy festival cycle. Leviticus 23 will get you off on the right foot.

Now that we have seen how Messiah and His early followers observed the Father's Divinely appointed times, and we have seen the list of appointed feasts, we also see that something is missing in this festival cycle. Now an entirely new question, one of glaring omission, has arisen:

5
WHY DO WE CELEBRATE CHRISTMAS?

Response:

"Because it is the birth of Christ!"

The Truth:

Nobody knows when Messiah was born. There *is* a reason we celebrate it, but it's not anything you would expect. Let's just dive right in.

Christmas is pagan. Not just pagan, but sickly and perversely pagan. The symbolism is nothing short of pornographic. The day and season are incorrect. The rituals are one hundred percent idolatrous. It's quite possibly the single greatest example of the old cliché "hiding in plain sight".

Let's start with two basic facts before we get started into this breakdown.

The first and foremost thing we need to keep in mind is that the Father *never once* commanded, sanctioned, hinted at or even politely asked that we celebrate His Son's birthday. This is a fact. Read the bible front to back and you will not find a single mention of it. Additionally, you will not find an instance of *any* Israelite's birthday being celebrated. In the ancient Hebrew culture, it was seemingly a non-issue.

I offer logic. Ponder this for a moment: the Father tells us that Yeshua is "His only begotten Son" and also tells us that "This is My beloved Son, in Whom I'm well pleased". If the Father wanted us to honor His "only begotten Son, in Whom He is well pleased" by celebrating His birthday, I'm all but positive we would find that somewhere in the bible.

Next basic fact: we have no proof of when His birthday actually was. We do have a few clues to work with, but they in no way lead us to December 25th. For example, we're told there was no room at the inn. This is definitely not because everyone was in town for Christmas. In fact, we can be reasonably certain it was not in winter for we're told in Luke 2:8 that there were Shepherd's tending their flock in the field by night. The Shepherd's in Israel did not tend their flocks by night in the winter months because of the cold...their sheep were kept in the fold. Why was every room taken? It was because everyone was in town for a *feast day*. The latest a feast day will ever occur is in late September/early October. Tabernacles (Sukkot) is decidedly considered the most likely date amongst scholars. Additionally, Bethlehem is less than five miles from Jerusalem. During one of these feasts where all were required to attend, every room in every lodge for miles around Jerusalem would have been occupied, thus He was born in a temporary shelter. Again, these are just clues we have to work with, and there are some great studies to be found out there concerning this. That said, the fact is we're *not told* when He was born.

So we see that we're not commanded to celebrate His birthday, nor do we have any scriptural examples of it being observed, nor do we even know when He was in fact born. Where then do we arrive at a birth celebrated worldwide on December 25th?

I submit to you facts, from Alexander Hislop and his incredibly well-researched work, "The Two Babylons":

"And first, as to the festival in honor of the birth of Christ, or Christmas. How comes it that the festival was connected with the 25th of December? There is not a word in the Scriptures about the precise day of His birth or the time of year when He was born. What is recorded there implies that at what time so ever His birth took place, it could not have been on the 25th of December. At the time that the angel announced His birth to the shepherds of Bethlehem, they were feeding their flocks by night in the open fields. Now...the climate of Palestine...the cold of the night, from December to February, is very piercing, and it was not the custom for the shepherds of Judea to watch their flocks in the open fields later than about the end of October. It is in the last degree incredible, then, that the birth of Christ could have taken place at the

end of December" (p. 91-92).

"Indeed, it is admitted by the most learned and candid writers of all parties that the day of our Lord's birth cannot be determined, and that within the Christian Church no such festival as Christmas was ever heard of till the third century, and that not till the fourth was far advanced did it gain much observance. How, then, did the Romish church fix on December 25th as Christmas-day? Why, thus: Long before the fourth century, and long before the Christian era itself, a festival was celebrated among the heathen, at that precise time of the year, in honor of the birth of the son of the Babylonian queen of heaven; and it may fairly be presumed that, in order to conciliate the heathen, and to swell the number of the nominal adherents to Christianity, the same festival was adopted by the Roman church, giving it the name of Christ. This tendency on the part of Christians to meet paganism half-way was very early developed" (The Two Babylons, p. 92-93).

"Upright men strove to stem the tide, but in spite of all their efforts, the apostasy went on, till the church, with the exception of a small remnant, was submerged under pagan superstition. That Christmas was a pagan festival is beyond all doubt. The time of the year, and the ceremonies with which it is still celebrated, prove its origin. In Egypt, the son of Isis, the Egyptian title for the queen of heaven, was born at this very time, 'about the time of the winter solstice.' The very name by which Christmas is popularly known among ourselves -- Yule-day -- proves at once its Pagan and Babylonian origin. 'Yule' is the Chaldee name for an 'infant' or 'little child'; and as the 25th of December was called by our Pagan Anglo-Saxon ancestors 'Yule-day,' or the 'Child's day,' and the night that preceded it 'Mother-night,' long before they came in contact with Christianity, that sufficiently proves its real character. Far and wide, within the realms of paganism, was this birthday observed. " (Hislop, p. 93-94).

The Babylonian queen of heaven and her son, eh? Now that we know that December the 25th was a sacred day commemorated by the pagans long before Messiah's birth, it begs the question, what was so important about December the 25th?

The winter solstice. This pagan feast was all about the sun. A short crash-course in solstices reveals the winter solstice to be the time that the sun is furthest from the earth and the days are at their shortest. History reveals that the early pagans, as well as most ancient peoples were amazing astronomers. By charting the sun's progress across the sky and using logical reasoning, they were able to determine when the Sun would start its progress back towards warmer weather and longer days. Thus, the winter solstice was celebrated as the sun's birthday.

"In the year 274 Aurelian declared the god -- now called **<u>Deus Sol Invictus</u>** *-- the official deity of the Roman Empire; he built a splendid temple of the sun in Rome, and* **<u>set the sun's birthday celebration on December 25</u>***, the date* **<u>then accepted for the winter solstice</u>** *(also in his solar character the birthday of Mithras). In the time of Constantine the cult of Deus Sol Invictus was still at its height, and the portrait of the sun-god was on the coins of Constantine. With his defeat of Licinius in A.D. 323 he became the uncontested ruler of the empire (323-337) and was free to openly accept Christianity....Likewise it must have been in this time and with the intent to transform the significance of an existing sacred date that the birthday of Jesus... was placed in Rome on December 25th, the date of the birthday celebration of Sol Invictus" (Jack Finegan, "Myth and Mystery"; Baker Books, 1989).*

In Rome the feast was also know as Saturnalia, for they celebrated it also to their agricultural God Saturn. The idea was that if they appeased their God of Agriculture, when the sun returned for the growing season Saturn would bless their crops.

Now we know who celebrated this pagan festival and we know why they celebrated it. So the important question now is... *how* did they celebrate it? This is sure to be an eye-opener.

The ancient Greek historian Lucian in his dialogue entitled "Saturnalia" wrote of the festival as it was observed in his day (125CE-180CE). His description included human sacrifice, widespread intoxication, going from house to house while singing naked and rape as well as other sexual licentiousness.

It is well documented that in the 4th century CE, Christianity imported the Saturnalia festival hoping to convert the pagan masses. The church was highly successful in this venture, by and large thanks to promises to the pagans that they could continue to celebrate Saturnalia as Christians.

I briefly have to add the following excerpts, simply because we need to be aware of these things. We just discussed the anti-Semitism of the church, so this fits right in:

In 1466CE, Pope Paul II and the Catholic Church observed a most horrible rite for the amusement of his Roman citizens. Pope Paul II forced Jews to race *NAKED* through the streets of the city.

"Before they were to run, the Jews were richly fed, so as to make the race more difficult for them and at the same time more amusing for spectators. They ran... amid Rome's taunting shrieks and peals of laughter, while the Holy Father stood upon a richly ornamented balcony and laughed heartily."(David I. Kertzer, The Popes Against the Jews: The Vatican's Role in the Rise of Modern Anti-Semitism, New York: Alfred A. Knopf, 2001, p. 74.)

As part of Saturnalia throughout the 18th and 19th centuries, rabbis in Rome were forced to wear clownish outfits and march through the city streets to the jeers of the crowd, having all kinds of projectiles thrown at them. When the Jewish community of Rome sent a petition in1836 to Pope Gregory XVI asking him to end the annual Saturnalia abuse of the Jews, he responded, *"It is not opportune to make any innovation."(Kertzer)*

On December 25, 1881, in an event known as the "Warsaw Pogrom", Christian leaders spread a false rumor that two Jewish men had been caught pick- pocketing in the church and then proceeded to whip the Polish masses into Anti-Semitic frenzies that led to riots across the country. In Warsaw 12 Jews were brutally murdered, huge numbers maimed and many Jewish women were raped. Two million rubles worth of property was destroyed. This event left over 1,000 Jewish families financially devastated.

Christmas was (and is) very anti-Semitic. These are lesser known facts, but facts nonetheless. Let's move on to better known customs and rites of Saturnalia. You'll be surprised to see how many still today pervade Christmas celebrations everywhere.

Christmas Caroling

Though not as common today as it was not so long ago, it is iconic to say the least. It is certainly still cemented in pop-culture, being portrayed in most of, if not all Christmas movies, TV shows, books and plays. We have already seen its origins above. Running naked from house to house singing songs.

Mistletoe

Much like caroling, it is not as common a practice today as it was in the last 200 years, but it also remains iconic. Its origins are many and varied, but by most accounts it is a fertility rite, hence "kissing under the mistletoe". Many sources also cite references that the white gooey sap on the branches of the plant represent…well, the sun-god's seed. That "seed" was thought to bring fertility to the barren womb.

Yule Log

This one is pornographic. In some ancient cultures it represented a phallic idol and was burned in the fire for 12 days with a fertility sacrifice offered in the fire every day. In other various cultures it represented a child being sacrificed; it being burned on the eve of the equinox was somehow meant to account for the festival (now Christmas) tree "magically" appearing in the house the following morning.

12 days of Christmas

See "Yule Log" above. A sacrifice a day for 12 days.

Gift Giving

In most all descriptions that can be found of any pre-Messiah December 25th festival, gift giving was a staple.

Gifts under the Tree

The tree was revered and worshipped as a god in many cultures. Think briefly about what you have to do Christmas morning to retrieve your gift from under the tree…yes, you have to get on your knees and bow to it. For the gifts that get shoved way back under the tree, you get to go full-prostrate.

Wreath

The wreath is also a fertility symbol…a *female* fertility symbol. It goes hand in hand, so to speak, with the Christmas tree…the *Male* fertility symbol. Let's leave it at that.

Christmas Tree

"The Christmas tree, as has been stated, was generally at Rome a different tree, even the fir; but the very same idea as was implied in the palm-tree was implied in the Christmas fir; for that covertly symbolized the new-born God as BAAL-BERITH, 'Lord of the Covenant,' and thus shadowed forth the perpetuity and everlasting nature of his power, now that after having fallen before his enemies, he has risen triumphant over them all. Therefore, the 25th of December, the day that was observed at Rome as the day when the victorious god appeared on earth, was held as the Natalis invicti solis, 'The birth-day of the Unconquerable Sun.' Now the Yule Log is the dead stock of Nimrod, deified as the sun-god, but cut down by his enemies; the Christmas tree is Nimrod redivivus -- the slain god come to life again"
(Hislop, "The Two Babylons")

From Shattered Paradigms:

One of the symbols most closely associated with Asherah was a tree. The ancient Canaanites and Phoenicians viewed the tree as a symbol of fertility. A symbol of male fertility. This is not a joke. (Keep that name, "Asherah" in mind -author)

The purpose of the fertility tree in ancient times was to display the symbols of fertility.

The pole, balls, and tinsel (phallus, testes, semen) represented various aspects of male fertility, while wreaths were always made in a circle to represent female fertility.

From Compton's Interactive Encyclopedia, 1997; under heading "Christmas":

"Trees and decorations. Ancient, pre-Christian (pagan) winter festivals used greenery, lights, and fires to symbolize life and warmth in the midst of cold and darkness. These usages, like gift giving, have also persisted."

So the tree was worshipped in all manner of ways, down to the most grotesque form where the pagans bowed before it, imagining it to be the male reproductive organ. The following is why I asked you to remember the name "Asherah". The goddess Asherah was symbolized by trees, and worshipped as such. Guess what? The scriptures have something to say about worshipping Asherah and her symbolic trees, also known as "Asherim" (plural).

1Kings 14: *[15]"For YHWH will strike Israel, as a reed is shaken in the water; and He will uproot Israel from this good land which He gave to their fathers, and will scatter them beyond the Euphrates River, **because they have made their Asherim, provoking YHWH to anger**.* (emphasis mine)

So they set up their Asherim, and that *provoked YHWH to anger*. King Asa knew what to do about that…repent.

1Kings 15: *[12] And he banished the perverted persons from the land, and **removed all the idols that his fathers had made**. [13] Also he removed Maachah his grandmother from being queen mother, **because she had made an obscene image of Asherah**. And Asa cut down her obscene image and burned it by the Brook Kidron.* (emphasis mine)

Repentance. Turning back. Destroying what's wrong and performing what's right. Returning to fidelity. It seems that the Father's views on this subject are very clear.

Exodus 34: *[12]"Watch yourself that you make no covenant with the* *inhabitants of the land into which you are going, __or it will become a snare in your midst.__*

13"But rather, you are to tear down their altars and smash their sacred pillars __and cut down their Asherim__

14—for you shall not worship any other Elohiym, for YHWH, whose name is Jealous, is a jealous Elohiym— (emphasis mine)

See also Deuteronomy 7:5 and 12:3.

Jeremiah 17: *2As they remember their children, so they remember their altars __and their Asherim, by green trees__ on the high hills.* (emphasis mine)

There are about 17 more Asherim/Asherah references, but I think you get the idea. There is one more scripture I want you to see. It is a perfect description of the Christmas tree, *exactly* as we know it today, forbidden by the Father:

Jeremiah 10: "__*Do not learn the way of the Gentiles*__*; do not be dismayed at the signs of heaven, for the Gentiles are dismayed at them. 3 For the customs of the peoples are futile; for one __cuts a tree from the forest__, the work of the hands of the workman, __with the ax__. 4 __They decorate it with silver and gold; they fasten it with nails and hammers So that it will not topple.__* (emphasis mine)

I have seen more pastoral commentaries on this passage than most any other I have yet researched. Almost all of their responses can be summed up thus: "There are many who say Jeremiah 10:3 is condemning the use of Christmas trees. These people (patronizing tone implied) take this verse completely out of context, ignoring the rest of the chapter, which is obviously talking about idols."

I'm almost speechless. But not quite...

No kidding. It *is* all about idols. That's the whole point. Is this intentionally misleading? Or is it simply a case of not being able to see the idolatry for the trees? See what I mean about the words of men twisting and discarding the word of the Father? That paraphrased quote was from *many* different pastors…who obviously don't know what idolatry is (Exodus 20:4) or that the command against it still applies to us (1John 5:21, 1Thes. 1:9, Rev. 21:8)

Well, we've beaten the tree issue to death now, but we did amass a substantial number of witnesses concerning the pagan (and disgusting) roots of the Christmas tree. Let's finish this off with jolly old St. Nick.

Santa Claus

This is another one of those head-scratchers. If you ever stop to think about it, it soon becomes mind boggling. What does a "jolly old elf" have to do with our Father or Messiah? I mean, isn't Santa in a sense some sort of god? All-seeing, all-knowing, rewarding the good and punishing the bad? The reason that he has some strange similarities to a god is because he *is* one. In a sentence, he is Thor, the Norse god of thunder. We're going to have more witnesses than just one sentence, however.

The alleged origin of Santa Claus as we now know him, is that he is *supposedly* based on an incredibly selfless Catholic known as Saint Nicholas who lived in the 4th century CE. I use the words "alleged" and "supposedly" with good reason:

"Nicholas' existence is not attested by any historical document, so nothing certain is known of his life except that he was probably bishop of Myra in the fourth century. …"   *("Nicholas, Saint" Encyclopedia Britannica 99)*

"Nicholas, Saint (lived 4th century), Christian prelate, patron saint of Russia, traditionally associated with Christmas celebrations. The accounts of his life are confused and historically unconfirmed."   *("Nicholas, Saint" Microsoft Encarta Encyclopedia 99)*

Unfortunately, very little is known about the real St. Nicholas. Countless legends have grown up around this very popular saint, but very little historical evidence is available. (Del Re, Gerard and Patricia. The Christmas Almanac. New York: Random House, 2004, p. 130)

In 1969, the final nail in the coffin to the feeble fable of St. Nicholas was officially hammered down. Despite the fact St. Nicholas is among Roman Catholicism's most popular and venerated "Saints," Pope Paul VI officially decreed the feast of Saint Nicholas removed from the Roman Catholic calendar. UPI Wire Services reported **that St. Nicholas and forty other saints <u>were deleted because "of doubt that they ever existed."</u>** *("Pope Marches 40 Saints Off Official Church Calendar."; UPI Wire Services.)*

Because the saint's life is so unreliably documented, Pope Paul VI ordered the feast of Saint Nicholas dropped from the official Roman Catholic calendar in 1969. ("Santa Claus" Microsoft Encarta Encyclopedia 99)

I think it very safe to say that Santa is not based on St. Nicholas, since the evidence points to the fact that he never even existed. So where did he come from?

The vast majority of Santa researchers (they *do* exist) agree that the many strange traits of Santa were borrowed from Norse mythology.

"Sinterklaas was adopted by the country's English-speaking majority under the name Santa Claus, and his legend of a kindly old man was united with old **Nordic folktales of a magician who <u>punished naughty children and rewarded good children with presents</u>***." ("Santa Claus" Encyclopedia Britannica 99)*

"Some Santa researchers associate Santa with the Norse "god" of Odin or Woden. Crichton describes Odin as <u>**riding through the sky on an eight-legged, white horse name Sleipnir.**</u> *(Santa originally had eight reindeer, Rudolph was nine). Odin lived in Valhalla <u>**(the North)**</u> and had a <u>**long white beard**</u>.*

Odin would __fly through the sky during the winter solstice (December 21-25) rewarding the good children and punishing the naughty.__" (Crichton, Robin. Who is Santa Claus? The Truth Behind a Living Legend. Bath: The Bath Press, 1987, pp. 55-56)

"Thor was the god of the peasants and the common people. He was represented as an __elderly man, jovial and friendly, of heavy build, with a long white beard.__ His element was the fire, __his color red.__ The rumble and roar of thunder were said to be caused by the rolling of his chariot, for he alone among the gods never rode on horseback but drove in __a chariot drawn by two white goats (called Cracker and Gnasher)__. He was fighting the giants of ice and snow, and thus became the Yule-god. He was said to __live in the "Northland" where he had his palace among icebergs.__ By our pagan forefathers he was considered as the cheerful and friendly god, never harming the humans but rather helping and protecting them. The fireplace in every home was especially sacred to him, and __he was said to come down through the chimney into his element, the fire.__"
(Guerber, H.A. Myths of Northern Lands. New York: American Book Company, 1895, p. 61)

It is not ironic that Thor's symbol was a hammer. Santa is indeed a toymaker, is he not? It should be noted that Thor's helpers were elves that were skilled craftsman as well, much like Santa's elves. It was Thor's elves that crafted his infamous, magical hammer.

I think we've dismantled the heresy of Santa Claus. He was an ancient god, and thanks to many factors, remains one today. I do want to cover one last little Santa tradition that I think we should all be well aware of before we trod through another Christmas season. Namely, the tradition of placing children in Santa's lap is a picture perfect replica of what many ancient pagans did for the god Molech: child sacrifice. There are a great many scholars who place Santa's origins in Molech.

The historical (and archeological) fact of the matter is, there was an ancient religious cult that was centered on sacrificing the first born to the god Molech. The manner in which it was done is horrific. They had a large metal statue, be it bronze or iron and it was built hollow on the inside. When performing a sacrifice, they would build a fire inside the statue, heat it until it was glowing *RED hot* and then set the child into its lap, amidst its open arms. Now picture Santa, in his bright *RED* suit, accepting children into his lap and open arms.

Deuteronomy 12: *[31] You shall not behave thus toward YHWH your Elohiym, for every abominable act which YHWH hates they have done for their gods; for they even **burn their sons and daughters in the fire to their gods**.*(emphasis mine)

As I've said before, look at it however you wish. I'm just stating the facts. We all at least deserve the facts so we can make our own decisions.

I want to offer one last bit of reasoning. Have you ever stopped to think what we must do in order to keep this myth alive? We must *lie* to our children for the first several years of their life. Ponder this: to keep Christmas alive, we must lie to our children about something that does not exist. Yet they can see this nonexistent thing *with their own eyes* on every street corner, in every mall, on every TV show and in every movie throughout every holiday season. When they are old enough to be told they were lied to, and that this thing that they can see with their own eyes does not actually exist...we want to start teaching them about Elohiym. Something they *cannot* see with their own eyes... and then we expect them to believe us. What are we going to say?

"You know I wouldn't lie to you...right?"

Just think about it.

Anyway, we have seen that the custom of keeping Christmas was instituted by the Roman Catholic Church, and is in no way commanded or even mentioned by the scriptures our entire belief structure is based upon. This point, that the Catholics are the true harbingers of this pagan, idolatrous "holiday" is a very important one to make. One would think that those who knowingly instituted a rite that breaks nearly every commandment of the Father would go to some extent to try and cover-up this fact. One would *think* such, but one would be *wrong*:

EXTERNALS OF THE CATHOLIC CHURCH, 1917, page 134, authored by John F. Sullivan

SOME CHRISTMAS CUSTOMS

"When we give or receive Christmas gifts, and hang green wreaths in our homes and churches, how many of us know that we are probably observing pagan customs? We do not wish to assert that they are not good customs; but they undoubtedly prevailed long before Christian times. The Romans gave presents on New Year's Day, and our bestowing of gifts at Christmas is a survival of that practice, as well as a commemoration of the offerings of the Magi at Bethlehem. The Yule-log, a feature of Christmas in old England, goes back to the days of the pirate Norsemen. Holly and mistletoe and wreaths of evergreen have been handed down to us by the Druids. And even our friend Santa Claus, that mysterious benefactor of our childhood days, existed in one form or another long before Christianity had attributed his virtues to St. Nicholas; for the god Woden, in Norse mythology, descended upon the earth yearly between December 25 and January 6 to bless mankind.

But, pagan though they be, they are beautiful customs. They help to inspire us with the spirit of "good will" even as the sublime services of our Church remind us of the "peace on earth" which the Babe of Bethlehem came to bestow. May that spirit fill the heart of each of us on every Christmas Day!"

There you have it. Open acknowledgement of Christmas' idolatrous roots. And yet, "Pagan as they may be, they're still beautiful customs!"

It is my sincere desire that you see the connection here. I pray that this open admission from the Catholics, that they have force fed you paganism, will move you to consider the magnitude of this situation. YHWH our Elohiym has issued, time and again, a no compromise command to avoid pagan idolatry. So do we do as the Catholics say? Or as the One who Created us, and holds our eternal fate in His hands, commands?

We have seen here an example of blatant transgression of the commandments in favor of a pagan holiday. This would lead us to wonder if this is not the *only* holiday to which this has happened.

6

WHY DO WE CELEBRATE EASTER?

Response:

"In honor of Christ's resurrection."

The truth:

Easter has absolutely *nothing* to do with Messiah's resurrection. There *is* a commanded Holy Day within the festival cycle that has *everything* to do with Messiah's resurrection, but Easter is completely devoid of meaning in a scriptural sense. It's actually specifically forbidden by the scriptures. We'll get to that. Let's just start at the beginning and go from there.

First, let's take a look at Lent. Now, you protestant believers out there are probably thinking "I don't celebrate Lent". Indeed we may not, but the truth of the matter is that our celebration of Easter was given to us by the Catholic Church. Therefore, we are going to cover all aspects as it pertains to Catholicism's influence on our holiday practices.

The following is again an excerpt from the excellent book, "The Two Babylons", originally written in 1858 by Alexander Hislop:

*"Whence, then, came this observance? The forty days abstinence of Lent was directly borrowed from the worshippers of **the Babylonian goddess [Astarte / Ishtar]**. Such a Lent of forty days, 'in the spring of the year,' is still observed by the Yezidis or Pagan Devil-worshippers of Koordistan, who have inherited it from their early masters, the Babylonians."*

"Such a Lent of forty days was held in spring by the Pagan Mexicans, for thus we read in Humboldt, where he gives account of Mexican observances: 'Three days after the vernal equinox .... began a solemn fast of forty days in the honour of the sun."

"Such a Lent of forty days was observed in Egypt, as may be seen on consulting Wilkinson's Egyptians. "

"Among the Pagans this Lent seems to have been an indispensible preliminary to the great annual festival <u>in commemoration of the death and resurrection of Tammuz</u>, which was celebrated by alternate weeping and rejoicing, and which, in many countries, was considerably later than the Christian festival, being observed in Palestine and Assyria in June, <u>therefore called the 'month of Tammuz</u>;' in Egypt, about the middle of May, and in Britain, sometime in April. <u>To conciliate the Pagans to nominal Christianity, Rome, pursuing its usual policy, took measures to get the Christian and Pagan festivals amalgamated</u>, and, by a complicated but skillful adjustment of the calendar, it was found no difficult matter, in general, <u>to get Paganism and Christianity -- now far sunk in idolatry -- in this as in so many other things, to shake hands</u>.

"Originally, even in Rome, Lent, with the preceding revelries of the Carnival, was entirely unknown; and even when fasting before the Christian Pasch was held to be necessary, it was by slow steps that, in this respect, it came to conform with the ritual of Paganism. What may have been the period of fasting in the Roman Church before the sitting of the Nicene Council does not very clearly appear, but for a considerable period after that Council, we have distinct evidence that it did not exceed three weeks. The words of Socrates, writing on this very subject, about A.D. 450, are these: 'Those who inhabit the princely city of Rome fast together before Easter three weeks, excepting the Saturday and Lord's day.' But at last, when the <u>worship of Astarte</u> was rising into the ascendant, steps were taken to get the whole Chaldean Lent of six weeks, or forty days, made imperative on all within the Roman empire of the West. The way was prepared for this by a Council held at Aurelia in the time of Hormisdas, Bishop of Rome [514-523], <u>about the year 519, which decreed that Lent should be solemnly kept before Easter</u>. It was with the view, no doubt, of carrying out this decree <u>that the calendar was, a few days after, readjusted by Dionysius.</u>" (The Two Babylon's, 1858, Alexander Hislop, second American edition, 1959, published by Loizeaux Brothers, pages 106, 107.)

The legend of Tammuz states that he was killed by a wild boar when he was forty years old. Hislop points out elsewhere in his book that forty days, a day for each year Tammuz had lived on earth, were set aside to "weep for Tammuz". The forty days were meant for mourning; through this mourning they hoped to gain Tammuz' favor so that he would come forth from the underworld and cause spring to begin. Ever wonder why we have an Easter ham? It's because a ham killed Tammuz, and eating one is exacting revenge on the beast that killed him.

You may be surprised to find that the bible actually has something to say *specifically concerning* this weeping for Tammuz. Ezekiel was taken in a vision to Jerusalem, where the Father showed him the many great abominations the House of Israel was committing with idols and the worship of false gods.

Ezekiel 8: *[12] Then He said to me, "Son of man, have you seen what the elders of the house of Israel do in the dark, **every man in the room of his idols**? For they say, 'YHWH does not see us, YHWH has forsaken the land.'" [13] and He said to me, "Turn again, and **you will see greater abominations that they are doing.**" [14] So He brought me to the door of the north gate of YHWH's house; and to my dismay, women were sitting there **<u>weeping for Tammuz.</u>*** (emphasis mine)

I find it fascinating that this very observance is recorded in the scriptures. I find it even more fascinating that the Father called it "an abomination" even *greater* than the *elders of Israel worshiping idols in the temple*.

The Father makes it clear throughout scripture that we are His bride and as such we participate in a marriage covenant. He also makes it clear that worshipping false gods and idols is adultery against Him and places us in violation of that covenant. The church now teaches us that it is fine to participate in these rituals the Father Himself calls adultery so long as we "do it for Him". I've heard it said many times that faithfulness to the Covenant was required by "that mean old God in the old testament". I think we've been snowed into a disconnect from scriptural reality. Let's put this in terms that are a little more personal:

Do you consider yourself a mean old wife/husband because you expect fidelity from your spouse? Secondly, do you foresee a day anywhere in the future that you will come to love your wife/husband so much that you release them from their covenant of fidelity to you?

Just think about it. Our fleshly marriage covenant is a mirror of our spiritual marriage covenant. The Father has made that pretty clear. Claiming we observe these Pagan rites "in His honor" is probably not going to go over well with Him.

This study of Lent brings us naturally to the pagan holiday of Ishtar. I mean Easter. I would like to guide your attention back to the excerpt from "The Two Babylons" above. Notice how the forty days of Lent were in preparation for Tammuz' *resurrection* on the day of Ishtar/Astarte. Those two names are one and the same, and yes, they are also the forerunner to the name "Easter".

Good Friday is the beginning of the end of this pagan-drenched season, with Easter Sun-Day wrapping up this spring festival. Right out of the gate, there are some serious problems with Good Friday alone. The concept of a Friday crucifixion and a Sun-Day resurrection in no way add up to three days in the tomb. The scriptures plainly state Messiah was raised up on the *third* day.

Matthew 16: *[21] From that time Yeshua began to show to His disciples that He must go to Jerusalem, and suffer many things from the elders and chief priests and scribes, and be killed, and be **<u>raised the third day</u>**.*

Mark 9: *[31] for He taught His disciples and said to them, "The Son of Man is being betrayed into the hands of men, and they will kill Him. And after He is killed, **<u>He will rise the third day</u>.</u>** "*

Luke 9: *[22] saying, "The Son of Man must suffer many things, and be rejected by the elders and chief priests and scribes, and be killed, **<u>and be raised the third day</u>**. "* (emphasis mine)

See also Matthew 17:23, 20:19, Mark 10:34, Luke 13:32, 18:33, 24:7, 24:46, Acts 10:40 and 1Corinthians 15:4.

You may be like me in that I never took the time to do the math concerning a Friday crucifixion.

Matthew 27: *[45] Now from the sixth hour until the ninth hour there was darkness over all the land. [46] And **<u>about the ninth hour</u>** Yeshua cried out with a loud voice, saying, "Eli, Eli, lama sabachthani?" that is, "My Elohiym, My Elohiym, why have You forsaken Me?"*
*[50] And Yeshua cried out again with a loud voice, **<u>and yielded up His spirit</u>**.*
(emphasis mine)

He was then taken and placed in the tomb before evening (Luke 23:53-54). If He was in the tomb right before sundown, which would have been necessary since sundown marked the beginning of a High Sabbath (that being the required Sabbath on the first day of Unleavened Bread) and if it was indeed on a Friday, then the numbers don't add up. Friday at dark to Saturday at dark is 24 hours. Saturday at dark to sunrise Sun-day morning is 12 hours. So by Catholic reckoning He was in the tomb a day and a half (36 hours) before He was raised. Above I have listed twelve scriptural verses saying He was to be raised *on* the third day. Yet the whole of the Christian faith has been misled to observe a rite in which He was resurrected early on the *second day*. I do not understand how this has been missed all of these years. The facts were right in front of us.

As you'll remember from an earlier chapter, Messiah was scripturally proven to be our *Passover* lamb. I've not seen one scripture where He's been called our Easter egg, nor have I seen any proof of Him being our Easter Bunny. In the year 32 CE, the year He was crucified, Passover began on Thursday, not Friday. Scripture tells us He died in the 9th hour, which is the same time the final Pesach (Passover) lamb was slain in the temple. That would be Thursday, April the 14th, 32CE at 3 o'clock in the afternoon. Therefore He was in the tomb by Thursday evening, which puts Him there Thursday night to Friday night (24 hours) and Friday night to Saturday night (24 hours). There we have two *full* days and nights. Thus, He could have risen any time after dark on Saturday evening and it would have been *on* the third day. It all fits perfectly if we simply look at the scriptures and historical facts of the matter. A quick side note: there are some who claim a Wednesday crucifixion, believing He must be in the tomb three *full* days and nights. Scripture does not say that. It says He rose *on* the third day. In that line of thought, if He were indeed in the tomb three full days and nights, that would have Him rising on the *fourth day*. That directly contradicts the dozen or so scriptural witnesses that claim He rose on the *third day*. Regardless, even if it were proven to me it was indeed a Wednesday crucifixion, I can live with that. We just simply *cannot* let this "Good Friday" stand. It is quite simply wrong. The facts and numbers do not allow for it.

All of this now brings us to Easter Sun-day, the day in which we supposedly celebrate the resurrection of our Messiah. First of all, I'm not saying that celebrating His resurrection is a bad thing. It is in *How* we celebrate it that the problem arises.

The scriptures do not call the day of His resurrection Easter. It was actually on the Feast of First Fruits.

Leviticus 23: *[10]"Speak to the sons of Israel and say to them, 'When you enter the land which I am going to give to you and reap its harvest, then you shall bring in the* **sheaf of the first fruits** *of your harvest to the priest.*

[11]'He shall **wave the sheaf before YHWH for you to be accepted***; on the day after the Sabbath the priest shall wave it.* (emphasis mine)

The description of First Fruits is given in Deuteronomy.

Deuteronomy 26: *[1]"Then it shall be, when you enter the land which YHWH your Elohiym gives you as an inheritance, and you possess it and live in it,*

[2]that you shall take some of the first of all the produce of the ground which you bring in from your land that YHWH your Elohiym gives you, and you shall put it in a basket and go to the place where YHWH your Elohiym chooses to establish His name.

[3]"You shall go to the priest who is in office at that time and say to him, 'I declare this day to YHWH my Elohiym that I have entered the land which YHWH swore to our fathers to give us.'

[4]"Then the priest shall take the basket from your hand and set it down before the altar of YHWH your Elohiym.

[5]"You shall answer and say before YHWH your Elohiym, 'My father was a wandering Aramean, and he went down to Egypt and sojourned there, few in number; but there he became a great, mighty and populous nation.

[6]'And the Egyptians treated us harshly and afflicted us, and imposed hard

labor on us.

[7]'Then we cried to YHWH, the Elohiym of our fathers, and YHWH heard our voice and saw our affliction and our toil and our oppression;

[8]and YHWH brought us out of Egypt with a mighty hand and an outstretched arm and with great terror and with signs and wonders;

[9]and He has brought us to this place and has given us this land, a land flowing with milk and honey.

[10]'Now behold, I have brought the first of the produce of the ground which You, O YHWH have given me.' And you shall set it down before YHWH your Elohiym, and worship before YHWH your Elohiym;

[11]and you and the Levite and the alien who is among you shall rejoice in all the good which YHWH your Elohiym has given you and your household.

First Fruits is an offering to be brought before the Father that acknowledges that all of the abundance they would experience was given by Him alone. It was to be presented as per Torah, so that they might be *accepted.* Now, there aren't many of us who are farmers today; more importantly, the place He chose to be honored with this offering is currently unavailable to us for use in any worship. It is the temple mount in Jerusalem and is currently occupied by the "Dome of the Rock", which is a Muslim shrine. This by no means suggests we shouldn't observe the required assembly for this Feast however, as it was commanded as a perpetual statute. Moreover, this Feast also points to our Messiah.

1Corinthians 15: *[20]But now Messiah has been raised from the dead, **<u>the first fruits</u>** of those who are asleep.*

[21]For since by a man came death, by a man also came the resurrection of the dead.

[22]For as in Adam all die, so also in Messiah all will be made alive.

*[23]But each in his own order: **<u>Messiah the first fruits</u>**, after that those who are Messiah's at His coming.* (emphasis mine)

First Fruits was celebrated on the first day of the week, Sunday, after the first Sabbath, that being Saturday after the first day of Passover. Our Messiah was resurrected on the Feast of First Fruits. Many hold that He rose early on Sunday morning, but scripturally speaking its far more likely He rose on Saturday evening, just after dark (the end of the Sabbath). This technically does start Sunday, being twilight on Saturday night. In any event, He was resurrected as First Fruits of those asleep on the day Israel celebrates the Feast of First Fruits.

This is an actual, scripturally sanctioned *holy day*, not a pagan-named heresy we now call a *holiday*. The only scriptural mention you will ever find of the name Easter is within older King James Versions of the bible. Virtually all recent translations from any publisher have corrected all mentions of Easter to the correct rendition of Passover (**Strong's G3957 - pascha**). So where does the name Easter come from?

The answer to that question is somewhat complex, but it very well documented historically. It all starts with Nimrod.

Genesis 10: *[8] **Cush begot Nimrod**; he began to be a mighty one on the earth. [9] He was a mighty hunter before YHWH; therefore it is said, "**Like Nimrod** the mighty hunter before YHWH." [10] And the beginning of his kingdom was Babel, Erech, Accad, and Calneh, in the land of Shinar. [11] from that land he went to Assyria and built Nineveh, Rehoboth Ir, Calah, [12] and Resen between Nineveh and Calah (that is the principal city).*

Nimrod figured prominently in what is commonly known as the "Great Mystery Religion" of Babylon (Hislop, The Two Babylons). When he finally died, his wife Semiramis saw to it that he remained prominent in the religion, deifying him as the Sun-God. With this he became known throughout various cultures as Baal, Bel, Baalim and Molech amongst many others. Semiramis was adulterous and highly idolatrous; when she later conceived and bore a son, she named him Tammuz. Claiming he had no human father, she said he was the promised seed and savior (sound familiar?). In essence, her dead husband Nimrod impregnated her and then he himself was reborn in the flesh. Thus Semiramis was both Tammuz' wife and mother. It's really weird and confusing. Semiramis came to be worshipped as much if not more so than Tammuz. He became the Sun-deity and she in turn became the Queen of Heaven, Mother of Creation and also became the Goddess of the Moon and Fertility. She was called Eostre, Astarte, Ostera, Wife of Baal, Ashtaroth and Eastre. The "Mother Goddess" was frequently worshipped as the "goddess of fertility"…a sort of Mother Nature and goddess of spring, sexual love and re-birth. Sexual orgies and temple prostitutes were often used in her worship in attempting to gain her favor. For reference, simply look to any dictionary or encyclopedia. I will recount a few short excerpts below.

"Easter. The name is derived from Eostre, the name of a goddess whose festival was celebrated at the vernal equinox; her name shows that she was originally the dawn-goddess." –Oxford English Dictionary

"Our name Easter comes from Eostre, an ancient Anglo-Saxon goddess, originally of the dawn. In pagan times an annual spring festival was held in her honor." –Compton's Encyclopedia

As you can see, Easter is thoroughly pagan in its origin. The rites that Christianity has observed throughout the centuries all derive directly from the worship of Nimrod, Tammuz and Semiramis (Ishtar/Eostre/Easter). I should point out once again that Nimrod/Tammuz was deified as the sun-god. Have you ever been to a sunrise service on Easter Sun-day? What did we do? We sat, *facing east, awaiting the rising sun* (a resurrecting Tammuz being re-born), supposedly to celebrate Messiah's resurrection. Let's not forget this important fact: the forty days of weeping for Tammuz culminated in *Tammuz' resurrection.* So in ancient times we had a 40 day fast leading up to a sunrise service to memorialize Tammuz' resurrection, and now, at the exact same time every spring we have…well, you get the picture. Did you know the Scriptures have something to say about this as well? It is found in the very same section of Ezekiel where we saw the women weeping for Tammuz. Interesting they should be mentioned one right after the other, is it not?

Ezekiel 8: *[13] And He said to me, "Turn again, and you will see greater abominations that they are doing." [14] So He brought me to the door of the north gate of YHWH's house; and to my dismay, __women were sitting there weeping for Tammuz.__*
[15] Then He said to me, "Have you seen this, O son of man? Turn again, you will see greater abominations than these." [16] So He brought me into the inner court of YHWH's house; and there, at the door of the temple of YHWH, between the porch and the altar, were about twenty-five men __with their backs toward the temple of YHWH and their faces toward the east, and they were worshiping the sun toward the east.__ (Emphasis mine)

Additionally, it is highly unlikely that Yeshua rose with the sun at dawn on Sun-day morning. Why is that? Because scripture tells us that when the women arrived in the dark of early Sun-day morning, He was already gone (John 20:1). Scripture does not tell us exactly when He rose, but with our new understanding of the Hebrew roots and life of our Messiah, we can postulate that He probably rose just after the end of the Sabbath, when His Sabbath rest had ended and darkness had finally settled on the land. Regardless, the scriptural fact is that the women arrived before dawn, and He was already gone. So where does the sunrise service originate?

"The custom of a sunrise service on Easter Sunday can be traced to ancient spring festivals that celebrated the rising sun." (New Book of Knowledge; 1978)

With all of that now thoroughly researched, it's time for the bonus round. The million dollar question is: what do eggs and rabbits have to do with Yeshua's resurrection? The answer is: ABSOLUTELY NOTHING. They do however have everything to do with sex and fertility. So what does fertility have to do with Messiah's resurrection? See previous answer. Here's the truth about bunnies:

"The hare, the symbol of fertility in ancient Egypt, a symbol that was kept later in Europe... Its place has been taken by the Easter rabbit" (Encyclopedia Britannica, 1991 ed., Vol. 4, p. 333).

A great many off-color jokes have been made throughout the years about the vigorous reproductive ability of rabbits. It is no coincidence that our observance of Easter today still holds all of these seemingly unrelated symbols, symbols that originated in the pagan observance centered on spring and re-birth. Hence, Easter finds its ritual near the spring equinox, when the plants begin to "revive" and start to grow once again. It's all about fertility. That's it. Therefore it is no stretch of the imagination to guess where the eggs came from. In addition to being obvious symbols of fertility, they also find basis in the pagan legends once again. The fable of Astarte (again, Eostre/Ishtar/Easter) states that she was born from an egg floating in the water. It is also documented in the early spring festival bearing her name, Ishtar worshippers celebrated with eggs dipped in sacrificial blood and orgies. She *was* the fertility goddess after all. If she had existed I'm certain she would have thoroughly enjoyed it.

So there you have it, Easter decoded. It really didn't need to be "decoded" however, merely researched. The pagan origins of Easter are obvious, blatant and too numerous to be dismissed. When confronted with such information, the clergy never fail to respond with "but we do it for Jesus now". I can't speak for you, but I haven't seen a single instance where "Jesus" asked any of us to do *anything* pagan for Him. I know I'm throwing a lot at you, but these are the facts. We have to know the facts. Do we want to continue on in ignorance and adultery? If we truly love the Father shouldn't we desire to make these things right and honor Him by doing what *He's* asked for, instead of what the Church at Rome has asked for? Do we still need convincing that it is indeed the Catholic Church that has instituted these rites? It's ok if we do, because we still have more proof:

"The use of temples, and these dedicated to particular saints, and ornamented on occasions with branches of trees; incense, lamps, and candles; votive offerings on recovery from illness; holy water; asylums; holidays and seasons... are all of pagan origin and sanctified by their adoption into the Church." (Cardinal John Newman, *An Essay on the Development of Christian Doctrine*, London: Basil Montague Pickering,1878; 373)

"Practically everything Protestants regard as essential or important they have received from the Catholic Church... The Protestant mind does not seem to realize that in accepting the Bible and observing the Sunday, in keeping Christmas and Easter, they are accepting the authority of the spokesman for the church, the Pope." (Our Sunday Visitor; February 5, 1950)

We have seen the idolatry in our "holidays" now with our own eyes and the church openly admits its implication in the adoption of this pagan idolatry. We should be careful to avoid idolatry:

Revelation 21: *[8]* *But the cowardly, unbelieving, abominable, murderers, sexually immoral, sorcerers, **idolaters**, and all liars **shall have their part in the lake which burns with fire and brimstone, which is the second death.*** "
(emphasis mine)

So now that we see that the church is responsible for adopting idolatrous holidays and ignoring the Holy days prescribed by scripture, we simply have to ask:

WHY DO WE ASSEMBLE ON SUNDAY?

Response:

"Because it's the lord's day".

The truth:

Your pastor is correct about this. Christianity assembles on Sunday, because it is the lord's day. The problem is… it's not the lord you think it is. It is a pagan lord. We're talking idolatry here.

*"Biblical Sabbath observance within the church continued until the time of Constantine when Sunday, the **Lord's day** (a name given to the first day of the week **in honour of the Roman Emperor-literally 'imperial day'**) was **substituted for the Sabbath**. The church council of Nicea in 325 "Widened the breach between Christianity in Judaism by forbidding the celebration of the Christian Sabbath on Saturday and tried to prevent the coincidence of Easter and Passover."* (The New Standard Jewish Encyclopedia, p.214)

So we see that history records for us the beginnings of Sun-day worship. It was commanded in honor of the Roman Emperor, and *replaced* the Sabbath spoken of in the bible. So when was the actual Sabbath spoken of in scripture observed? Saturday, the *seventh* day of the week.

Genesis 2: *²By the **seventh day** Elohiym completed His work which He had done, and **He rested on the seventh day** from all His work which He had done.*

*³Then Elohiym **blessed the seventh day and sanctified it**, because in it He rested from all His work which Elohiym had created and made.* (emphasis mine)

A quick look at a calendar reveals that Saturday is the seventh day of the week, and Sun-day is the first. Saturday is the end of the scriptural week.

Some contend that there has been so many centuries since Constantine instituted the change in the day of worship, that we cannot be sure what day to worship on, therefore it does not matter. This is not true. There has only been one change in the calendar since these events, and it did not change the ordering of the days of the week, merely the date:

"Since His (Yeshua's) time, there has been an abundance of recorded history that verifies the chronology up to the present. Even when the secular calendar was changed by Pope Gregory XIII in 1582 and ten days were eliminated to bring the seasons back into alignment, only the date was changed, not the day of the week; i.e., Oct. 4th, 1582 was followed by Oct. 15th. The Sabbath has not been mislabeled as another day of the week."   (Warren Bowles, Christianity Reconsidered; Montgomery-Porter Publishing, 2004)

So what was this talk about Constantine changing the Sabbath to Sun-day? We see that it was already being honored amongst the Pagan Romans as the day of their Emperor (lord), but there was something else very alluring about Sun-day to Constantine…he was a sun worshiper. Sunday worship was instituted in honor of the Sun-god…hence its name: SUN-day. I'll let the references do the talking:

"Constantine called the sun-deity: "unconquered sun, my companion." His edict in the year 321 legislated the "venerable day of the Sun" to be a rest day. This rest was commanded in honor of the sun, and not in honor of Messiah.   (C.J. Koster, Come Out of Her My People; Institute for Scripture Research (PTY) Ltd 2008)

"While claiming to be a Christian, Constantine maintained the title 'Pontifus Maximus', the high priest of Paganism. His coins were inscribed "SOL INVICTO COMITI" which means 'committed to the invincible sun'."   (Richard M. Rives, Too Long in the Sun; p.66 Charlotte Partakers Publications, 2001)

This is where it gets interesting. At this point, many will make the argument "How do we know that those sources aren't tainted? How do we know they aren't just trying to sway us to their own agenda?"

The answer is found in the words of the Catholics themselves. Constantine created the Catholic Church in 325 CE at the Council of Nicea.

We have just seen outside sources claiming that the Catholics are the ones who have given us this command to keep the Sun-day Sabbath. But what do the Catholics have to say about this charge that has been leveled against them? You would be amazed:

"Prove to me from the bible alone that I am bound to keep Sunday holy. There is no such law in the bible. It is the law of the holy Catholic Church alone. The bible says, 'remember the Sabbath day to keep it holy.' the Catholic Church says, No. By my divine power I abolish the Sabbath day and command you to keep holy the first day of the week. And, LO! The entire civilized world bows down in reverent obedience to the command of the holy Catholic Church."

(Thomas Enright, CSSR, President, Redemptorist College (Roman Catholic), Kansas City, MO., Feb. 18th 1884)

"Sunday – fulfillment of the Sabbath. Sunday is expressly distinguished from the Sabbath which it follows chronologically every week; for Christians its ceremonial observance replaces that of the Sabbath...

The Sabbath, which represented the completion of the first creation, has been replaced by Sunday which recalls the new creation inaugurated by the Resurrection of Christ...

(The Catechism of the Catholic Church Section 2 Article 3 (1994)

"But you may read the Bible from Genesis to Revelation, and you will not find a single line authorizing the sanctification of Sunday. The Scriptures enforce the religious observance of Saturday, a day which we never sanctified."

(Cardinal James Gibbons, The Faith of Our Fathers; Ayers Publishing, 1978; p. 108)

"Q. Which is the Sabbath day?

A. Saturday is the Sabbath day.

Q. Why Do we observe Sunday instead of Saturday?

A. We observe Sunday instead of Saturday because the Catholic Church transferred the solemnity from Saturday to Sunday."

(The Convert's Catechism of Catholic Doctrine, 1957; p.50)

"If Protestants would follow the Bible, they should worship God on the Sabbath day which, by God, is Saturday. In keeping the Sunday, they are following a law of the Catholic Church."

(Chancellor Albert Smith for Cardinal of Baltimore Archdiocese, letter dated February 10, 1920)

"Question: Have you any other way of proving the Church has power to institute festivals of precept?

Answer: Had she not such power, she could not have done that in which all modern religionists agree with her, she could not have substituted the observance of Sunday the 1st day of the week, for the observance of Saturday the 7th day, a change for which there is no Scriptural authority."

(Stephen Keenan, Catholic—Doctrinal Catechism 3rd Edition: 174)

"Practically everything Protestants regard as essential or important they have received from the Catholic Church... The Protestant mind does not seem to realize that in accepting the Bible and observing the Sunday, in keeping Christmas and Easter, they are accepting the authority of the spokesman for the church, the Pope."

(Our Sunday Visitor; February 5, 1950)

"Thus the observance of Sunday by the Protestants is a homage they pay, in spite of themselves, to the authority of the (Catholic) Church."

(Louis Gaston Segur, Plain Talk about the Protestantism of To-Day; London: Thomas Richardson and Son, 1874; p. 213)

"It was the holy Catholic Church that changed the day of rest from Saturday to Sunday, the 1st day of the week. And it not only compelled all to keep

Sunday, but at the Council of Laodicea, AD 364, anathematized those who kept the Sabbath and urged all persons to labor on the 7th day under penalty of anathema."

(Catholic Priest T. Enright, CSSR, Kansas City, MO)

"CHRISTIANS must not judaize by resting on the Sabbath, but must work on that day, rather honouring the Lord's Day; and, if they can, resting then as Christians. But if any shall be found to be judaizers, let them be anathema from Christ."

(Council of Laodicea, 364CE; Canon XXIX)

"I have repeatedly offered $1000 to anyone who can furnish any proof from the Bible that Sunday is the day we are bound to keep...The Bible says, "Remember the Sabbath day to keep it holy," but the Catholic Church says, "No, keep the first day of the week," and the whole world bows in obedience."

(Catholic Priest T. Enright, CSSR, lecture at Hartford, KS, Feb 18, 1884)

"Sunday is our mark of authority...The [catholic] Church is above the Bible, and this transference of the Sabbath observance is proof of that fact."

(Catholic Record; September 1, 1923)

"But since Saturday, not Sunday, is specified in the Bible, isn't it curious that non-Catholics, who claim to take their religion directly from the Bible and not from the Church, observe Sunday instead of Saturday? Yes, of course, it is inconsistent; but this change was made about fifteen centuries before Protestantism was born, and by that time the custom was universally observed. They have continued the custom even though it rests upon the authority of the Catholic Church and not upon any explicit text in the Bible. That observance remains as a reminder of the Mother Church from which the non-Catholic sects broke away—like a boy running away from home but still carrying in his pocket a picture of his mother or a lock of her hair."

(John A. O'Brien, The Faith of Millions: the Credentials of the Catholic

Religion Revised Edition; Our Sunday Visitor Publishing, 1974; p. 400-401)

Man, oh man…Can it get any more arrogant?

Believe it or not, yes. Yes it can.

"We hold upon this earth the place of God Almighty."

(Pope Leo XIII, *Praeclara Gratulationis Publicae "The Reunion of Christendom"*, June 20, 1894)

"The Pope is of so great dignity and so exalted that he is not a mere man, but as it were, God, and the vicar of God."

("Pope," *Ferraris' Ecclesiastic Dictionary*)

"Not the Creator of the Universe in Genesis 2:1-3, but the Catholic Church can claim the honor of having granted man a pause to his work every seven days."
(S.C. Mosna, *Storia della Domenica*; 1969: p. 366-367)

I think we can now safely say "It cannot get any more arrogant than that". So, apparently, the Catholics feel they can change the appointed times of Elohiym, because they have *"taken His place upon this earth"*.

I'm wincing at the thought of even *quoting* that…I'm just waiting on the lightning bolt.

So, I think we have done all the damage to the idea of a "Sunday Sabbath" that we can do for one day. Sunday is not the Sabbath, no matter how we slice it. We should be honoring our Creator's day of rest. This brings us to the other facet of this Sabbath situation: how we observe it.

The unfortunate truth of the matter is that even Christians who observe Sun-day as their Sabbath do not observe it according to our Creator's instructions. The scriptural Sabbath is honored by resting. No work and no chores. It is a day of *rest* for us. Since we are commanded not to work, by proxy comes the other instruction for the Sabbath: we can't put any one else to work either. As in, we can't spend money on the Sabbath. No shopping, no eating out…no money can exchange hands. I offer witnesses:

Exodus 20:   [8]*"**Remember the Sabbath day, to keep it holy.**" [9]"Six days you shall labor and do all your work,*

[10]*__but the seventh day is a Sabbath of YHWH your Elohiym; in it you shall not do any work__, you or your son or your daughter, your __male or your female servant__ or your cattle or your sojourner who stays with you.*

[11]*"For in six days YHWH made the heavens and the earth, the sea and all that is in them, __and rested on the seventh day; therefore YHWH blessed the Sabbath day and made it holy__.*   (emphasis mine)

You see that Elohiym specifically addresses the idea of making our servants work. Sure, very few of us have servants…but what is the more proper term for the waiter or waitress at our Sun-day lunch spot?

Servers.

Many people try to get around this in any way they can. They will try and say that these employees are not their servants, etc. However, Nehemiah does us a service by specifying that we cannot spend money on the Sabbath:

Nehemiah 10: [31]*As for the peoples of the land who bring wares or any grain on the Sabbath day to sell, __we will not buy from them on the Sabbath or a holy day__; and we will forego the crops the seventh year and the exaction of every debt.* (emphasis mine)

That's pretty clearly stated, but to leave no margin for error, let's look at another section concerning the Sabbath in chapter 13:

Nehemiah 13: [15]*In those days I saw in Judah some who were treading wine presses on the Sabbath, and bringing in sacks of grain and loading them on donkeys, as well as wine, grapes, figs and all kinds of loads, and __they brought them into Jerusalem on the Sabbath day So I admonished them on the day they sold food__.*

*¹⁶Also men of Tyre were living there who imported fish and all kinds of merchandise, **and sold them to the sons of Judah on the Sabbath**, even in Jerusalem.*

*¹⁷Then I reprimanded the nobles of Judah and said to them, **"What is this evil thing you are doing, by profaning the Sabbath day?***

*¹⁸"Did not your fathers do the same, so that our Elohiym brought on us and on this city all this trouble? **Yet you are adding to the wrath on Israel by profaning the Sabbath**."*

*¹⁹It came about that just as it grew dark at the gates of Jerusalem before the Sabbath, **I commanded that the doors should be shut and that they should not open them until after the Sabbath. Then I stationed some of my servants at the gates so that no load would enter on the Sabbath day**.*

²⁰Once or twice the traders and merchants of every kind of merchandise spent the night outside Jerusalem.

*²¹Then I warned them and said to them, "Why do you spend the night in front of the wall? If you do so again, I will use force against you." **From that time on they did not come on the Sabbath**.*

*²²And I commanded the Levites that they should purify themselves and come as gatekeepers **to sanctify the Sabbath day** For this also remember me, O my Elohiym, and have compassion on me according to the greatness of Your lovingkindness.* (emphasis mine)

Scripture stands as our witness. Elohiym set-apart the Sabbath day, instructed us to rest upon it, let everyone else rest as well *and* told us that it is a statute that stands forever. Historical documents have also stood witness to the "transference" of the Sabbath, and at that, straight from the horse's mouth. The Catholics fully claim responsibility for the substitution of Elohiym's Sabbath to that of the sun-god. They seem to be quite proud of it.

So, should we honor Elohiym on Sun-day? I think the answer is clear. Let me show you a scripture that clearly states we cannot mix worship before Elohiym. We cannot observe Pagan traditions, and pretend to do it for Him:

Deuteronomy 12: *³⁰beware that you are not ensnared to follow them, after* *they are destroyed before you, and that you do not inquire after their gods, saying, '**How do these nations serve their gods, that I also may do likewise?**' [31] **You shall not behave thus toward YHWH your Elohiym**, for **every abominable act which YHWH hates they have done for their gods**; for they even burn their sons and daughters in the fire to their gods.* (emphasis mine)

He makes it painfully clear with one sentence: "You shall not act like they did to their gods to Me". This isn't just about serving or worshiping other gods, it's about serving *our* Elohiym in the way that the *pagans served theirs*.

We have seen now very clearly and thoroughly that the early church has bastardized almost *everything* that the Father originally instructed us to do. The cards are starting to fall now…we're in danger of the whole house coming down. Where else have we been mislead?

8
WHY DO WE TITHE?

Response:

"Do not muzzle the ox while it's threshing."

-or-

"The worker is due his wages."

The truth:

The truth is that, for once, you pastor has actually quoted scripture to answer your question. The problem is that this is taken out of context and severely abused. This question serves its purpose far better if you set it up with this statement to your pastor first: "I think we should keep the law". Your pastor will respond "Oh, no. The law has been done away with." *That* is when you ask "Then why do you request my tithe?"

You see, the instruction to tithe is only found in the *law*. This is the very reason you should be asking this question. So the law is only done away with if it does not pay his salary? If it does, then that is *one* law that still applies? I've been taught by that very same man that only the ten commandments apply. The instruction for the tithe is not found in the ten commandments. So what's the deal here?

--------------------------------------\$--------------------------------------

If your preacher demands a tithe, if he stands at the pulpit Sun-day morning nearly begging for it, or shaming you to do it…he is robbing you. Point blank.

I suggest you bring him wheat, barley and new wine. Why? Because the *produce* of the land is the only thing ever commanded to be tithed.

This is where they start assigning things to modern "equivalents".

He will say "Well, we're not farmers now, so your produce is your paycheck". Additionally, He assigns himself to the position of a Levite, because the Tithe was only commanded to be given to the Levites. Indeed, it is also for the widow, the orphan and the poor, but in the sense of being "recompensed" for service to Elohiym, the Levites were the only ones specifically commanded to receive it and perform that service. Here's the problem: pastors have no authority *whatsoever* to assign themselves to the position of a Levitical priest. Only Elohiym Himself has the authority to make such a designation. There is not one single line of scripture that even hints that this instruction for the tithe has been transferred to anyone other than the Levites. So have our pastors set themselves above the Most-High? Have they assumed the authority of Elohiym Himself, and changed one of His commandments? According to scripture, they better *not* have:

Proverbs 30: *⁶ Do not add to His words,*
Lest He rebuke you, and you be found a liar.

Let's take a moment to look at why the Levites received the Tithe.

Numbers 18: *²⁴ For the tithe of the sons of Israel, which they offer as an offering to YHWH, I have given to the Levites for an inheritance; therefore I have said concerning them, '* ***They shall have no inheritance among the sons of Israel***.*'"* (emphasis mine)

The Levites received the tithe *because* they were granted *no inheritance* in the land. What does that mean? Why does that give them the right to the tithe? It means they were given no land, therefore they could not farm for its produce to feed themselves. They could not provide for their own sustenance, nor did they even have time. You see, when a Levite was "on duty" in the temple, he was offering sacrifices all day long, caring for the Holy utensils, the sacrificial fires etc., etc. A Levite's work was actually *serious manual labor* that lasted *all* day, *every* day. They couldn't have even held down a job if they had wanted to. Let me relate a short anecdote to you. I was once an assistant to the pastor at my church for a summer, in addition to being the praise and worship leader and assistant youth leader. Let me tell you from personal experience…our pastor did nothing all day, five days a week. The man could have easily held down a day job, simply because there was *nothing for him to do all week*.

Now, let me actually address your pastor's original response to the question. First, I'll show you the verses he gets it from:

1Cor. 9: *⁹For it is written in the Law of Moses, " YOU SHALL NOT MUZZLE THE OX WHILE HE IS THRESHING." Elohiym is not concerned about oxen, is He? ¹⁰Or is He speaking altogether for our sake? Yes, for our sake it was written, because the plowman ought to plow in hope, and the thresher to thresh in hope of sharing the crops.*

1Timothy 5: *¹⁸For the Scripture says, " YOU SHALL NOT MUZZLE THE OX WHILE HE IS THRESHING," and " The laborer is worthy of his wages."*

There is a ton of stuff to address here, so bear with me. First, and most importantly, Paul is *quoting Torah* (the law) to make a point:

Deuteronomy 25: *⁴" You shall not muzzle the ox while he is threshing."*

This is very much worthy of noting…how could a man who was so (supposedly) anti-law use the law to reinforce a point? Just keep that in the back of your mind as we move on. Secondly, he quotes something else, but it appears that it did not come from the Tanakh. The best chance it has of being from the Tanakh is being a paraphrase of Leviticus 19:13 or Deuteronomy 24:15. However, there is another source that fits the wording far better, as in, word for word:

Luke 10: *⁵Whatever house you enter, first say, 'Peace be to this house.' ⁶ If a man of peace is there, your peace will rest on him; but if not, it will return to you. ⁷Stay in that house, **eating and drinking** what they give you; **for the laborer is worthy of his wages**. Do not keep moving from house to house. ⁸Whatever city you enter and they receive you, **eat what is set before you**;*

Matthew 10: *⁹**Do not acquire gold, or silver, or copper for your money belts**, ¹⁰or a bag for your journey, or even two coats, or sandals, or a staff; for the **worker is worthy of his support**.*

Notice that Yeshua *specifically* says "Do *not* acquire gold, silver or copper for yourself, but eat what is set before you". So Yeshua is telling them that they shouldn't feel bad or indebted when their basic needs were met, but they are *not to profit* from those they are teaching. This is where we get into the "meat" of this subject. The reality of the situation is found within the context of who He was talking to. Who were they? The seventy that He had sent out into the land to proclaim the good news. Who was Paul? One similar to the seventy. Traveling throughout the world proclaiming the gospel. This provides for us the reality of their situation:

It's kind of hard to hold down a day job when you're traveling around the world from city to city constantly.

Especially with the lack of Leer Jets in ancient Israel, a person could spend *weeks* or even *months* on a boat, in a wagon, on a donkey or just simply walking. Sprinkle in some stoning, persecution and jail time, and you can begin to see why those who were *literally* laboring were worthy of the bread and wine that the people they stayed with set before them. This is a lesson in *context*. Modern religion has done its very best to hide the context of scripture from us, and has unfortunately accomplished it to a great degree. This is case in point. Do you know what your Pastor does all week? If you think it takes him a full week to prepare Sunday's three-scripture sermon and visit the occasional hospital room, you have been mislead. My father-in-law prepares a bible study twice a week that has more scripture and meat in it than you can get in church in 6 months of Sundays. He *still* has a day job, and refuses to accept a penny for teaching the Word of Elohiym. How can He possibly fit all that into a week? Because it doesn't take forty hours to prepare a study.

This is pushing us towards a point I want to make. Where do you see a house, a Cadillac and a Rolex in the above scriptures? What I see is food and drink. I see a *room* in somebody *else's* house. I see Yeshua *specifically* forbidding taking gold, silver and money. All that I see above is basic biological needs. This is what Paul was quoting to reinforce his point. It is very logically implied that he intended Yeshua's instruction on this subject to be the watermark for understanding the point he was trying to make. Yeshua said "do not take from them financially, but accept their food and shelter". All of this brings us to a mistranslation I would *love* to clear up from Paul's first letter to Corinth. It's found in 1Corinthians 9:

> 1Corinthians 9: *[11] If we sowed spiritual things in you, is it too much if we reap **material things** from you?*

So, what is the first thing that comes to mind when you hear the term "material things"? For me it's a house, a Cadillac and a Rolex. So this verse, at face value, very clearly seems to say "Give the man a healthy *salary*". *However*, according to the original Greek word, it should *instead* read "Give the man some healthy *celery*":

Material Things- Strong's G4559 - sarkikos

1) fleshly, carnal
    a) having the nature of flesh, i.e. under the control of the animal appetites

2) having its seat in the animal nature or aroused by the animal nature

There is not one single definition of this word for "Material things" that even comes close to meaning financial gain. Let me ask you something. Would hunger, thirst and shelter be considered carnal desires? Something our *flesh* needs? Something our basic human biology must have? Now, with that in mind, let's look once again at the words of Yeshua that Paul was directly quoting:

Luke 10: ⁷ *Stay in that house, **eating and drinking what they give you**; for the laborer is **worthy of his wages**.*

Suddenly we have corroboration. Makes a lot of sense, doesn't it? Paul wasn't saying to give them a career, he is simply restating Messiah's words: "Don't feel bad for accepting room and board, you deserve the food and accommodation they offer you".

Here's one more:

1Corinthians 9: ¹³ *Do you not know that those who perform sacred services eat the food of the temple, and those who attend regularly to the altar have their share from the altar? ¹⁴ So also the Master directed those who proclaim the gospel to get their **living** from the gospel.* (emphasis mine)

Ok, translation time again:

Living- Strong's G2198 - zaō

1) to live, breathe, be among the living (not lifeless, not dead)

2) to enjoy real life
    a) to have true life and worthy of the name
    b) active, blessed, endless in the kingdom of God

> **3) to live** i.e. pass life, in the manner of the living and acting
>   **a)** of mortals or character
>
> **4) living water**, having vital power in itself and exerting the same upon the soul

Do you see a single definition that even *begins* to allude to financial gain? Me either. According to the biblical scholars, it *literally* translates "So also the Master directed those who proclaim the gospel of eternal life to *gain eternal life themselves*. That just makes a ton of sense, doesn't it? Yeshua told us to lay up our treasures in Heaven. So for Paul to say here that "those who preach the gospel of everlasting life will *also have the reward of everlasting life*" is not out of place at all. It's not even a stretch of the imagination. It actually fits quite naturally. Especially considering the contrast Paul makes with the priests of the temple. The priests did their appointed work in the temple, offering sacrifices on behalf of the people. They in turn had rights to portions of that sacrifice. Paul and the apostles were laboring in the field of proclaiming the gospel of eternal life…the sacrifice of Yeshua…so they themselves had rights to their portion of Yeshua's sacrifice. What did Yeshua's sacrifice bring? Eternal life. See what I mean about keeping it in context?

Now, even *if* we take Paul's words at their seeming, face-value meaning in this particular instance, they do not contradict all of the scriptures we have yet looked at. To us "making a living" means that it's our job, career and lively hood. Considering who Paul was quoting, and the weight of all the other scriptures combined, this verse can just as easily read "the Master appointed those who proclaim the gospel to get their daily sustenance from the people they are teaching it to". In other words, they weren't going to starve or freeze to death, because Elohiym was going to provide food and shelter through His people.

Also important to note, in none of the above scriptures is it ever said that the people should give their *tithe* to these who were laboring in the gospel. Go and re-read it. Not one mention of the tithe. This very clearly seems to be regarding something to the effect of a "free-will offering". It is important to note what these people were doing for the apostles was *commanded in Torah*. Quite simply, we are commanded to never turn a brother away from our home or neglect giving them what their body requires to live (Deut 15:7, Leviticus 19: 9-10, 23:22 and Deuteronomy 24: 19-20,). That's not a part of the tithe, that's just a basic instruction from Torah. James understood this:

> James 2: *[14] What use is it, my brethren, if someone says he has faith but he has no works? Can that faith save him? [15] **If a brother or sister is without clothing and in need of daily food**, [16] and one of you says to them, " Go in peace, be warmed and be filled," **and yet you do not give them what is necessary for their body, what use is that?** [17] Even so **faith**, **if it has no works**, **is dead**, being by itself.*

Once again, the Tithe was *only* for the Levites and the Temple so far as "recompense" for Elohiym's work was concerned.

You see, sometimes translations are *very* tainted by their human translators. If there is one thing I have learned in my thirty-one years in this mortal coil, it's this: when *money* is involved, don't be surprised by *anything* that *anyone* is willing to do. You can look at me as a conspiracy theorist or a pessimist if you wish, but I prefer to look at this as being realistic. You don't have to look very far at all to see pastoral excess, monetary misappropriation and wanton waste. It makes headlines fairly frequently. We call it "fleecing the flock".

Here's the deal. I don't disagree that Paul states "a worker is due his wages", I merely disagree with the modern definition of "wages". Preachers can very well work a full time job. This is a fact. I know several, and I know what they do all week…and it's not much. When a pastor is receiving a salary, making a living that pays for his vehicles, vacations and anything else he does…somewhere there is a widow, an orphan or brother in need who *does not have that money*. Who do you think needs it more?

You see, pastors today claim the tithe as their due wage. The problem is that the tithe was never intended to be a "wage", it was intended to be a means of basic providence. Food, water and shelter. Once again, it was *only* for the Levites, the poor, the widowed and the orphaned. Never once does scripture say it is to go to anyone who teaches the word. You may provide for them if you wish, but not with your tithe.

Does your tithe go to that new 20 million dollar youth-center? Then you are being robbed, the widow, the poor and the orphan are being robbed, and *moreover*, Elohiym is being robbed. Do you really think the kids need an arcade game to play *more* than somebody needs food or the money to keep their electricity on? Many say, "well, we can do *both*". No, no you can't. Not with your *tithe*. If you want to give a free-will offering to go to that youth building and fill it with arcade games and ping-pong tables, that's fine by me. But do *not* give the money that belongs to the needy among you to that building, to the pastor, or to any other cockamamie thing the church has going. Give it to those who actually *need* it for the reason it was originally *commanded*: for the sustenance of the physical body and need for shelter.

The Levites, as a blood line, ceased to exist long ago. As did the *hard, manual labor* they performed 70 hours a week. Our pastors are not Levites.

We see that in this case there may be a motive to have you in church. Full pews lead to full offering plates. Are our church leaders fully disclosing everything that scripture entails? As we have just proven, in some cases they are not. So what if they were telling you what you wanted to hear? Imagine how many pews would be empty if the pastor were teaching something that didn't cater to our liking. It should be of concern to us what the preacher is teaching, when his salary and job security depend on pleasing our ears…and our hearts. Jeremiah and Yeshua have already told us that we can't trust our own hearts (Jer. 17:9, Matt 15:19, Mark 7:21). I know personally of a few pastors or teachers that found themselves out of a job when they shunned the doctrines of men and started teaching the truth of scripture. Therefore, we must scour the bible for its truth to see if the pastor's words line up with the word of Elohiym. This begs a *very* important question:

9
WHAT MUST I DO TO BE SAVED?

Response:

"Say the sinners prayer. Repeat after me." (Baptist)

"Be baptized in our tank." (Church of Christ)

"Confess in the confessional." (Catholic)

"Ask Jesus into your heart." (all denominations)

The truth:

…is hard to swallow. The reality of scripture is this: we cannot *do anything* to be "saved". The Father himself does the choosing on this matter, and there is *absolutely nothing* you or I can do about it.

Don't toss the book just yet…please. Just give me a few pages to scripturally prove this to you.

Yes, pre-destination is a touchy subject. Oh my heavens, I've seen this topic go off like an atomic bomb more than once. The issue is very important though. There is no need for us to delude ourselves in an attempt to feel better. Scripture speaks wholly and strongly about this subject. Let's not find ourselves fighting against Elohiym. Gamaliel understood the importance of this (Acts 5:39).

Let's get started by looking at some verses from Paul that speak of what it takes to be "saved":

Romans 8: *[28] And we know that Elohiym causes all things to work together for good to those who love Elohiym, to those who are called according to His purpose. [29] For those whom **He foreknew**, **He also predestined**, conformed to the image of His Son, so that He would be the firstborn among many brethren; [30] and these whom **He predestined**, He also called; and these whom He called, He also justified; and these whom He justified, He also glorified.*

I really don't know how that could be any clearer, but Deut. 19:15 requires two or three witnesses. I think we'll have several more than that…just to be safe.

Notice above that we're quoting from Romans 8. Keep in mind that this was a letter that Paul wrote, and did not have chapters and verse numbers. This next quote follows very shortly after the above words of Paul:

Romans 9: *[11] for though the twins were not yet born and had not done anything good or bad, so that Elohiym's purpose __according to His choice__ would stand, __not because of works but because of Him who calls__, [12] it was said to her, " THE OLDER WILL SERVE THE YOUNGER." [13] Just as it is written, " JACOB I LOVED, BUT ESAU I HATED. "*

Again, very clear. Paul uses the story of Jacob and Esau to illustrate this point about *predestination* that he is trying to make. Notice how it had nothing to do with their *actions* or even *feelings*…they were not yet even born. It says specifically that this was because of Elohiym's *choice*. Is this not fair? Is it unjust? It certainly seems so to us…but our ways are not the Father's ways. Paul addresses this question:

Romans 9: *[14] What shall we say then? **There is no injustice with Elohiym, is there? __May it never be__**! [15] For He says to Moses, " I WILL HAVE MERCY ON WHOM I HAVE MERCY, AND I WILL HAVE COMPASSION ON WHOM I HAVE COMPASSION." [16] So then it __does not depend on the man who wills or the man who runs__, but on Elohiym __who has mercy__. [17] For the Scripture says to Pharaoh, " FOR THIS VERY PURPOSE I RAISED YOU UP, TO DEMONSTRATE MY POWER IN YOU, AND THAT MY NAME MIGHT BE PROCLAIMED THROUGHOUT THE WHOLE EARTH. " [18] __So then He has mercy on whom He desires, and He hardens whom He desires__.*

I told you that this was a clear scriptural concept, but I also understand how hard to swallow this is. The problem is that we feel that *we* are in control of our own lives. For many of us that grew up in tough circumstances, we *need* to feel in control of our lives…for the feeling of helplessness is horrible. However, whatever our reasons, we *must* submit to the Creator. Paul addresses this as well:

Romans 9: *[19] You will say to me then, " Why does He still find fault? For who resists His will?" [20] On the contrary, __who are you, O man, who answers__* *back to Elohiym? The thing molded will not say to the molder, "Why did you make me like this," will it? ^{21} Or **does not the potter have a right over the clay**, to make from the same lump **one vessel for honorable use and another for common use**? ^{22} What if Elohiym, although willing to demonstrate His wrath and to make His power known, endured with much patience vessels of wrath prepared for destruction? ^{23} And He did so to make known the riches of His glory upon vessels of mercy, which He **prepared beforehand** for glory.*

So Paul pretty well lines this out completely. We were prepared beforehand for glory or wrath. One or the other. It has no bearing whatsoever whether we want it or run from it, it will stand as He *predestined.* It is very important to note that Paul is merely teaching a subject that was taught before…in the Tanakh:

Isaiah 45: ^{9}*"Woe to the one who quarrels with his Maker—An earthenware vessel among the vessels of earth! **Will the clay say to the potter**, 'What are you doing?' Or the thing you are making say, 'He has no hands'?*

We see here that Paul was clearly teaching a concept from the Tanakh. From this, we can glean a bit of information…this was no new concept. It has been around since the beginning. Just as Elohiym willed it.

Ephesians 1: ^{4}*just as **He chose us** in Him **before the foundation of the world**, that we would be holy and blameless before Him. In love ^{5} **He predestined us to adoption as sons** through Messiah Yeshua to Himself, **according to the kind intention of His will**,*

Paul clearly understood the implications of predestination. He either chose us, or He did not…and regardless of which, He did so before the foundation of the world. Let's look at a couple of more verses to back our premise.

Revelation 13: ^{8}*All who dwell on the earth will worship him, everyone whose name has not been **written from the foundation of the world in the book of life** of the Lamb who has been slain. ^{9} If anyone has an ear, let him hear. ^{10} If **anyone is destined for captivity, to captivity he goes**;*

Revelation 17: ^{8}* " The beast that you saw was, and is not, and is about to come up out of the abyss and go to destruction. And those who dwell on the earth, whose name has not been **written in the book of life from the foundation of the world**, will wonder when they see the beast, that he was* *and is not and will come."*

Often we forget the authorship of some of the scriptural text. Let us be diligent to keep in mind that the Revelation to John came from *Messiah Himself.* Messiah clearly states through John that if we are of the chosen, our name has been written in the book of life since the beginning of the world…since *creation.*

What we now have are three witnesses to establish this matter. We have our witness from the Tanakh in Isaiah, Jacob, Esau and Pharaoh. We have our Brit Chadasha witness in Paul and his reiteration of Elohiym's words through Isaiah, and finally, we have Messiah Himself teaching us that we were chosen before the beginning of time. I don't know what else can be said, so we will leave this as it is: scripturally confirmed.

Now that we have done that, I want to offer some words on the implications of this. First and foremost, I understand how incredibly freaky this idea is. We don't hold our life in our own hands. We don't control our own destiny. What is the point of doing good or evil if the end result doesn't change accordingly? Trust me friends, I totally understand.

However, take some comfort in logical reasoning. Do you desire to please the Father? Do you hate anything that dishonors Him, disrespects Him or dismisses Him? Then you are most likely one of His. As Paul clearly pointed out, some were made as vessels for glory, and some as vessels for wrath. Those who were appointed to wrath are not going to instinctively desire to do good. They were created to do what they do. If your desire is to do evil, you most assuredly don't even care about honoring the Father. I would venture to say you wouldn't even be reading this book. If you are reading this book then you are searching for answers…you are searching for the truth. What would cause you to search for the truth? The Father's Spirit, guiding you back to obedience. If the Father's Spirit abides in you, guiding you to search for His ways, then you have no reason to worry. In any event, we must remember Paul and Isaiah's words: who are we to say to our Maker, "Why have you created me thus?" the Father will do as He pleases, whether we like it or not.

Now, to discuss the idea of our actions. Some would now venture to say "If we don't have a choice, it's either death or life for me, why should I do good, why shouldn't I be promiscuous and chase money?"

We should do good because the good works of Elohiym were *also* prepared from the foundation of the world, that we might walk in them:

Ephesians 2: *⁸ For by grace you have been saved through faith; and that not of yourselves, it is the gift of Elohiym; ⁹ not as a result of works, so that no one may boast. ¹⁰ For we are His workmanship, created in Messiah Yeshua **for good works**, which **Elohiym prepared beforehand so that we would walk in them**.*

So you see, the good works were prepared beforehand for His elect. I will discuss that in more detail in just a moment, but first we have to clear up a mistranslation. It is the word "faith" found in verse 8. It could quite easily be translated as "faith*fulness*":

"Faith"-Strong's G4102 - *pistis*

> 2) fidelity, faithfulness
> > a) the character of one who can be relied on

You see, this word "pistis" is a Greek *action* word. It is not about thoughts or feelings, it requires *action*. This is where mistranslation can so drastically slant our understanding. In this case, it not only has changed something of action into emotional bliss, that misunderstanding in and of itself has misled us in respect to whom it applies. This verse is not about *our* faithfulness to the Father, it's about *His* faithfulness to us. Let's look at that real quick, *literally* translated:

Ephesians 2: *⁸ For by grace you have been saved through **faithfulness**; and that not of yourselves, it is the gift of Elohiym;*

Now doesn't that make more sense…it makes the *entire passage* make more sense. Notice what Paul says directly after "saved through faithfulness": that faithfulness is not *our* faithfulness…it's the *Father's*. Paul clearly states that it is His gift to us. That is your definition of grace, folks. He graciously chose us to be His through faithfulness. But, to what is He being faithful? We are benefitting from His faithfulness to what?

The covenant He made with Abraham, Isaac and Jacob.

Genesis 22: *[18]* ___In your seed all the nations of the earth shall be blessed,
because you have obeyed My voice.___ "

Genesis 26: *[3] Sojourn in this land and I will be with you and bless you, for
to you and to your descendants I will give all these lands, **and I will establish
the oath which I swore to your father Abraham**. [4] I will multiply your
descendants as the stars of heaven, and will give your descendants all these
lands; and by your descendants **all the nations of the earth shall be blessed**;
[5] because Abraham obeyed Me and kept My charge, My commandments, My
statutes and My Torah.* "

So you see, we are receiving the blessing that Elohiym promised through
His faithfulness to the oath that He made with Abraham. As Paul pointed
out, this leaves no room for us to boast. We didn't earn our election as His
children. We're merely reaping the benefit of the covenant He made with
Abraham.

So this finally brings us back to the concept of works. We can't boast in
our works…they did not get us chosen. But yet, there are still good works to
be performed. Why? If we are already chosen, why do them?

Why do you expect your children to be obedient to you, or you spouse to
be faithful?

The good works He prepared beforehand, that we should walk in them are
merely our duty as obedient children. We are not obedient to our Parents to
become their children, are we? We are already their children, and that not by
any *choice of our own*, but by *their* choice to *create us*. Does that make a
little more sense?

We are obedient because we *love* our parents, and want to *please them*.
Does He not call Himself our Heavenly *Father*? It's no wonder then, that He
tells us the only way to please Him is to *obey the instructions* He gave us.

Now, on the other side of the coin, remember when you disobeyed dad?
Remember when you didn't do that homework? He wasn't very pleased, was
He? What always came next?

Punishment.

With Punishment for disobedience in mind, it would make sense that we would need to know what the specific instructions *are* that we need to obey. There are a great many *differing* ideas of what instructions apply to us. These different definitions of sin can be found almost every corner of every town in the world on Sunday morning. Now we must ask:

10
WHY ARE THERE SO MANY DENOMINATIONS?

Response:

"They are all just different ways of worshiping God."

The truth:

Actually, they are all just different definitions of sin. Since we have already established the importance of avoiding sin (so we won't have to *die eternally*), this is a very important subject that strangely flies right under the radar. This subject is like the stealth bomber of theology.

It is widely considered and accepted that the differing denominations all just worship Elohiym differently. It is "understood" that they are all going to Heaven, they are just on "different paths" to get there.

Stop for a moment and take in the magnitude of that last sentence. I have had that said to me so many times that I couldn't even begin to count them. People generally accept that there are *different* paths to Heaven. Messiah disagrees completely:

Matthew 7: *[13]* " ___**Enter through the narrow gate**___*; for the gate is wide and the way is broad that leads to destruction, and there are many who enter through it. [14] For the gate is small and* ___**the way is narrow that leads to life**___*, and there are* ___**few who find it**___*.*

So, according to Yeshua, there are only two ways in *total* that we may walk. There is only *one way* and *one gate* to enter into life. This statement alone completely destroys the idea of there being "different paths" to "Heaven". According to an article I recently read, there are many, *many* paths to "Heaven" currently being used. Care to guess how many?

More than *thirty-eight thousand.*

That's a lot of paths. It would seem to me that many paths would tend to overlap each other…and kind of meld into one *wide, broad* way. Additionally, those 38,000 denominations are compromised of more than 2.25 *billion* people. That is 1/3 of the population of the entire earth. Yeshua said there was only *one narrow* way into the Kingdom, and very *few* who would find it. Something is amiss.

The bottom-line truth is that there are different denominations because nobody can agree on what they want to be sin. Yes, I just said what they *want* to be sin. I can say that with confidence because the bible only teaches that one thing is sin…and that is transgression of Torah. Every single denomination in the world disagrees with that. They all disagree over subjects like dancing, drinking, music, baptism and so on…the list goes on forever. Torah, however, is neatly divided into 613 commandments. Something just occurred to me. I've been told many times that "there's no way anyone could keep that many commandments".

So I've just had a thought:

Would we rather try and keep 613 commandments that are written down in black and white and reside in the bible in our hands?

Or try and sift through 38,000 denominational doctrines to decide which one best suits our idea of sin?

There are *sixty-two times* as many denominations as there are actual scriptural commandments. I don't know if you've ever seen your denominations set of rules, by-laws, etc…but I have, and there's a *lot more* there than 613 easy-to-read instructions for a better life. Let's just say, *very* conservative estimate, that there are 200 rules per denomination. That's 7,600,000 (seven million, six hundred thousand) different rules. Does that illustrate modern Christianities aversion to the simplicity of Torah's 613 instructions sufficiently?

I want to make a note here about these 613 instructions. The idea that there are 613 rules has been greatly overblown by pastors seeking to belittle the path that scripture teaches us to walk. It has been used as a way to polarize the "mean strictness" of Torah against the "do whatever you want, Jesus doesn't care" feel-good doctrine they offer in its stead. Well, for starters, we've already seen how mean and strict Torah is: take a nap on Saturday, party six times a year, and take care of the poor and needy. Secondly, they neglect to tell you that all 613 commandments do not apply to you. Are you a Levite? Then that right there is a huge chunk of the commandments out the window as far as your concerned. Is there a temple currently in Jerusalem? Then there's more you don't have to worry about. Are you the government in the land of Israel? Then no need to worry about all of those commandments for government. A quick note here. This is why when the pastor chides "then you stone people to death", you can confidently say "No, I don't. That's the government's job…you really should study the bible more". The point is, there are only a select number of the 613 instructions that apply to you. When you go and study Torah, you will see that for yourself, and in turn will see that there is nothing within them that is hard at all to do.

This is the bottom line truth: there are *not* "many different" paths to eternal life. There is only one "way"…and that's *His* "way".

"The Way"- Strong's H1870 – derek

-) road, way, path
-) manner, habit, way

The Hebrew word for "way" is 'derek'. There are only two scriptural uses of this word, as you can see from the definition. The literal meaning, as in an actual road or path, and the metaphorical meaning, as in our conduct or manner in which we act. Let's look at how it is used in scripture:

Exodus 18: [20] *And you shall **teach them the statutes and the Torah, and show them the way** (derek) in which <u>they must walk</u> and the <u>work they must do</u>. (emphasis mine)*

Proverbs 10: [17] <u>***He who keeps instruction is in the way***</u> *(derek)* <u>***of life***</u>, *But he who* <u>***refuses correction goes astray***</u>. *(emphasis mine)*

Proverbs 15: [10] *Grievous punishment is for him who* <u>***forsakes the way***</u> *(derek);* <u>***He who hates reproof will die***</u>. *(emphasis mine)*

Psalm 119: [1] *How blessed are those* <u>***whose way***</u> *(derek)* ***is blameless**, Who* <u>**walk in the Torah of YHWH**</u>. *(emphasis mine)*

Psalm 119: [35] ***Make me*** <u>***walk in the path***</u> *(derek)* ***of Your commandments**, For I delight in it. (emphasis mine)*

Psalm 119: [105] <u>***Your word***</u> *is a lamp to my feet And **a light to** <u>**my path**</u> (derek). (emphasis mine)*

Psalm 128: [1] *How blessed is everyone **who fears YHWH**,* <u>***Who walks in His ways***</u> *(derek). (emphasis mine)*

We see here what Yeshua was alluding to when He said "the way" is narrow, and few there be that find it. The scriptures we just read *scripturally* define, in inarguable terms what Elohiym's way (derek) is. It's His Torah. Now, let's think for a moment about the contrast Yeshua made between the narrow way and the broad. We've just proven the narrow way is Torah. Now, keep in mind that a contrast demands a positive and a negative. The narrow path to life is the positive. What is the negative? *Broad* is the path that leads to *destruction*. So if walking in the "narrow way" is keeping the Torah (law), then walking in the "broad way" is ignoring the Torah. So the broad way is sin, which we have already *scripturally* defined as *lawlessness*…or transgression of Torah. It all starts to come together doesn't it?

I've got another good scripture for you. Do you know what the early followers of Messiah, after His crucifixion, called their sect of Judaism?

Acts 24: *[14] But this I admit to you, that according to **"the Way" which they call a sect** I do serve the Elohiym of our fathers, **believing everything that is in accordance with the Torah** and that is **written in the Prophets**;*

The early followers called themselves "the way". We have just proven prior to this verse that "the way" of the Father is to obey His instructions as written in Torah. Now, for the bonus round: do you know who was speaking here in Acts 24?

Paul.

The man who *supposedly* spoke so defiantly against the Torah, testifying before government under oath that he follows with the sect (of Judaism) known as "the way", believing *"all that is in accordance with the Torah"*.

Now, why would this sect of Judaism call themselves the way? There are two reasons. You have just seen the first…that is what YHWH calls His Torah. The second reason is:

John 14: *[6] Yeshua said to him, "I am **the way**, and the truth, and the life; no one comes to the Father but through Me.*

So now the question is: why did Yeshua call Himself the way? Because He *was* the way. The Torah made flesh:

John 1: *[14] And **the Word became flesh** and **dwelt among us**, and we beheld His glory, the glory as of **the only begotten of the Father**, full of grace and truth.* (emphasis mine)

I know it says "word became flesh" and not "Torah became flesh".

Definition time:

The Word- Strong's G3056 - *logos*

> 2) the sayings of God
> 3) decree, mandate or order
> 4) of the moral precepts given by God
> 5) Old Testament prophecy given by the prophets
> 6) what is declared, a thought, declaration, aphorism, a   weighty saying, a dictum, a maxim

So Yeshua was the word made flesh, which is Torah. The word is the Torah. I've seen no other "moral precepts, dictums, maxims, decrees, mandates or orders" anywhere else in scripture. He also gave us three full witnesses to this matter. The one you have just seen here in the terminology of "the way", and he also called Himself the "truth" and the "life".

Guess what?

John 17: *[17] Sanctify them by Your truth. **Your word is truth**.* (emphasis mine)

Deuteronomy 32: *[46] he said to them, " Take to your heart all the words with which I am warning you today, which you shall command your sons to observe carefully, even **all the words of this law**. [47] For it is not an idle **word** for you; indeed **it is your life**.*

You see, scripturally, "the way", "the truth" and "the life" are all references to Torah. We have all the witnesses we need now. Yeshua said He was the Torah made flesh, John corroborated it and Paul testified to it *under oath*. Three witnesses. There are hundreds more, but that is for you to research. We have fulfilled the required Torah of Deuteronomy 19:15 on this subject.

So we see, there is only one "way" to the Father. In addition to that, according to scripture itself, it isn't even *one* of the 38,000+ man-made ways to get there. The only way is through His Messiah...through His

Torah. All of the denominations are built on their own idea of how to please the Father…and none are completely in line with scripture. The answer to our question, "why are there so many denominations", is simple: humans wish to deny the Torah. They favor their own set of rules over that of the Father. When we do away with the only instructions our Creator ever gave us, we open the gate for everyone to make their own rules. When we've done this, we have set the stage for "anything goes". When "anything goes", everything falls apart.

Now that we are nearing the conclusion of this book, it seems only fitting to address the misconceptions about death…the reality we will all face someday as we near the conclusion of our lives.

11

WHAT HAPPENS WHEN I DIE?

Response:

"You go to Heaven."

The truth:

…is that you merely go to sleep. You simply die, until the resurrection. Scripture clearly tells us that judgment comes *after* the resurrection (2Peter 3:7, Hebrews 9:27, John 5:27-29, also Matthew 10:15, 12:36, 12:41, 12:42, Luke 10:14, 11:31, 11:32, 1John 4:17, Revelation 14:7 and 2Corinthians 5:10).

We all know that scripture speaks extensively on the resurrection, but have you ever stopped to wonder how the idea that we "die and go to Heaven" and are *then* somehow resurrected to judgment co-exist? I know I sure did. If you die and go to Heaven, then you have already been judged. How then can one be judged again at the resurrection? The truth is, these two ideas (scripturally speaking) *cannot* co-exist. Now, I know that this is going to really bother some people, but hear me out…I offer scripture as my witness.

Psalm 13: *3 Consider and answer me, O YHWH my Elohiym; Enlighten my eyes, or I will sleep the **sleep of death**,*

John 11: *11 This He said, and after that He said to them, "Our friend **Lazarus has fallen asleep**; but I go, so that I may awaken him out of sleep." 12 The disciples then said to Him, "Master, if he has fallen asleep, he will recover." 13 **Now Yeshua had spoken of his death**, but they thought that He was speaking of literal sleep.*

This is very clear. When we die, we merely "sleep". Essentially, we will have no consciousness of anything until the resurrection. Let's look at a few more witnesses.

Acts 13: *³⁶ For David, after he had served the purpose of Elohiym in his own generation, __fell asleep__, and was laid among his fathers and __underwent decay__;*

Again, very clear. This points out graphically that dying is indeed going to "sleep". It speaks of David undergoing decay. Paul speaks on this subject in a couple of places as well.

1Corinthians 15: *¹⁸ Then also those who have __fallen asleep__ in Messiah __have perished__.*

1Thessalonians 4: *¹³ But I do not want you to be ignorant, brethren, __concerning those who have fallen asleep__, lest you sorrow as others who have no hope. ¹⁴ For if we believe that Yeshua died and rose again, even so Elohiym will bring with Him __those who sleep in Yeshua__.*

¹⁵ For this we say to you by the word of the Master, that we who are alive and remain until the coming of the Master will by no means precede those __who are asleep__. ¹⁶ For the Master Himself will descend from heaven with a shout, with the voice of an archangel, and with the trumpet of Elohiym. And the __dead in Messiah will rise first__.

There's no way around it. When we die, we merely have a cessation of consciousness *until* the return of Yeshua. It is then that we will be raised…just like Lazarus.

Let me offer you a couple of witnesses about sheol…the grave. Many believe when the wicked die, they go to hell. The word hell is derived from sheol…which literally just means the grave. As in dirt, ground and dust.

Proverbs 9: *¹⁸ But he does not know that __the dead are there__, That her guests are in the __depths of Sheol__.*

Ecclesiastes 9: *⁵ For the living know that they will die; But the __dead know nothing__,*

Ecclesiastes 9: *¹⁰ Whatever your hand finds to do, do it with your might; for __there is no work or device or knowledge or wisdom in Sheol__ where you are going.*

I just want to point out…that this is *King Solomon* talking. Elohiym told us that He blessed Solomon with *wisdom* greater than that of any man. Solomon tells us specifically that there is no consciousness when we die. He says there is no "knowledge or wisdom in the grave. The dead know nothing". If we went to heaven when we died, then I'm pretty sure we would know *something*.

There is really only one verse that is used to support the idea of life in Heaven *immediately* after death:

Luke 23: *[42] And he was saying, "Yeshua, remember me when You come in Your kingdom!" [43] And He said to him, "Truly I say to you, today you shall be with Me in Paradise."*

Ok, so it would *seem* that we have a snake in our boot. So is Yeshua saying that all of the scriptures we just read are incorrect? That Solomon didn't know what he spoke of? That Paul had somehow misunderstood the idea of death?

Or is it at all possible that there is another answer? One that doesn't go against the rest of scripture at all?

Let's go with option B. We just can't go against so many scriptural witnesses. Yeshua Himself said He came to establish the Torah and the Tanakh, not contradict it (Matt. 5:17). Also keep in mind what Paul said long after Messiah's death and ascension:

Romans 3: *[31] Do we then make void Torah through faith? Certainly not! On the contrary, **we establish Torah**.*
(emphasis mine)

Now, to the point at hand. Remember how I mentioned earlier that the original manuscripts did not have punctuation? What if this were simply a matter of comma placement?

It is translated to us as this:

"Truly, I say to you, today you shall be with Me in Paradise."

But look what happens when we move the comma:

"Truly, I say to you today, you shall be with Me in Paradise."

Keep in mind that it was *human translators* who originally decided where *they* thought the punctuation marks should go. It merely requires the replacement of one comma to rectify any seeming contradiction between Yeshua's statement here and what was previously written.

You know that saying "I'm telling you right now"?

Example:

"I'm telling you right now, the Cards are going to win the world series next year!"

Now, did I just say the Cards are winning next year's world series right *now*? Or did I merely make the statement *right now*, that *next year* they will win the series? Of course, there is much more certainty in Yeshua's words, but I think you see my point. With the rest of scripture considered (as it must all agree), I am certain Yeshua said "*I'm telling you right now friend, when you are resurrected, you will join me in Paradise.*"

Allow me to relay another, secular example to you. There is a story floating around out there about a teacher, who wishing to illustrate the importance of punctuation, wrote the following on the board:

"Woman without her man is nothing"

He then asked the students to punctuate it how they saw fit. The men all punctuated it as:

"Woman without her man, is nothing."

The women, of course, punctuated it thus:

"Woman; without her, man is nothing."

Whether this is a true story or not is meaningless. This thoroughly and clearly drives home the point of how punctuation can completely change the inferred meaning and understanding of a sentence. This is true even when that sentence is compromised of the exact same words, in the exact same order.

Scripture has clearly shown us the truth about the idea that we die and immediately go to be with Messiah. It just isn't so. The idea is based off of ancient pagan belief systems (see the Greek "Elysium", or "Elysian Fields"). Scripture stands defiantly against it. So why would we be taught about eternal paradise after death and before the resurrection, when scripture teaches no such thing? It makes us feel good. It's merely a feel-good thing. What do people like to do when they feel good?

Give.

Seriously, there are studies on this. Corporations are dead serious about money and they put tons of it into research in order to make tons more. Happy people have loose wallets. True story.

So now that scripture has provided for us the truth about the extended dirt-nap that we are all destined to take (but maybe not…look to the sky and hope), what is the truth about judgment? What will we face when we finally resurrect? What will we be judged by? What criteria? This is the ultimate question, is it not? Our eternity hangs in the balance of this one simple question.

We will be judged according to Torah. Of all things, The Brit Chadasha (NT) holds the scriptures that confirm that for us:

Revelation 20; *[11] Then I saw a great white throne and Him who sat upon it, from whose presence earth and heaven fled away, and no place was found for them. [12] And I saw **the dead**, the great and the small, standing before the throne, **and books were opened**; and another book was opened, which is the book of life; and **the dead were judged from the things which were written in the books, according to their deeds**. [13] And the sea gave up the dead which were in it, and death and Hades gave up the dead which were in them; and **they were judged**, **every one of them according to their deeds**. [14] Then death and Hades were thrown into the lake of fire. **This is the second death**, **the lake of fire**. [15] And if anyone's name was not found written in the book of life, he was thrown into the lake of fire.*

You notice that there were *books*…plural. Books were opened, and the dead were judged by the things written in the books according to their deeds. They were not judged by their thoughts, feelings, beliefs or convictions…they were judged by their *deeds*. So what books could possibly be opened that would hold the judgments of one's deeds? The only such books ever written: Genesis, Exodus, Leviticus, Numbers and Deuteronomy. The Torah. You'll notice (for reference) that the book of life was mentioned separate of the judgment books. Do you remember when the names were written into the book of life? From the foundation of the earth. Do you also remember when the good deeds (that we will be judged by) were prepared, that we should walk in them? Again, from the foundation of the earth. Interesting how these things all come to tie together, isn't it?

Now, back to the idea we touched on earlier about *eternal* punishment. Notice that it says the lake of fire is the second *death*. It doesn't say the second *life* of eternal punishment. It says the second *death*. Let's have a second witness to the second death:

Revelation 21: [8] *But for the cowardly and unbelieving and abominable and murderers and immoral persons and sorcerers and idolaters and all liars, their part will be in the lake that burns with fire and brimstone, which is __the second death__.*"

So what does that mean? I think it's pretty clear. Those who face the wrath of judgment will be tossed into the fiery lake, and once they have died in that fire…they're gone. That's it. I know this goes against common Christian theology, but is this conclusion not wholly backed by scripture? There is no everlasting, burning punishment in "Hell". Guess where the concept of "Hell" came from…again, Greco-Roman mythology. But why would pastors preach eternal agony when the scriptures merely teach that the evil perish?

It, wouldn't have anything to do with keeping us in church, would it? If we're in church, that offering plate is going to pass every Sun-day…and we don't want to be the one everyone sees it pass over do we? I know I sure didn't. Studies also show that guilt and fear are very profitable. This is very much along the lines of extortion and ransom:

Stay in church, because you don't want to burn in eternal agony forever and ever and ever…maybe even for all eternity, and the fire will never stop and the pain will never stop and the agony will never stop and it will be dark but fiery and evil like a horror movie but worse because it's for real and you're really there and Satan will be walking around and that's super scary and creepy and there are demons and worms and probably snakes and spiders there too…do you?

Let's take a quick look at the only scripture pastors really have to work with to support the idea of never-ending hell:

Isaiah 66: [22] *"For just as the new heavens and the new earth, which I make will endure before Me," declares YHWH, "So your offspring and your name will endure. [23] "And it shall be from new moon to new moon And from Sabbath to Sabbath, All mankind will come to bow down before Me," says the Master.[24] "Then they will go forth and look **<u>on the corpses</u>** of the men who have **<u>transgressed against Me</u>**. For their **<u>worm will not die and their fire will not be quenched</u>**; And they will be an abhorrence to all mankind."*

Ok, I know I let a lot of extra verse remain in there, but it was necessary to establish the context. Verse 22 establishes that this is about the end of days, thus about judgment…the New Heaven and New Earth are mentioned. Verse 23 is just icing on the cake, proving that when Yeshua returns, we will all be keeping the Sabbath (and not Sunday) as well as the new moon festivals…all scriptural Holy Days. Verse 24 is back to the point at hand. Our pastors use the verse *"their worm will not die and their fires not be quenched"* as their support for this eternal agony claim. However, there is one word that they skip over in this passage. The word I want you to notice is "corpses". What must happen to somebody in order to become a corpse? They have to *die*. So they will not be screaming and in agony for all of time…they will just *die*. According to Elohiym, speaking through Isaiah, those who transgressed against our Creator will die finitely (for good) in the second death, but their inanimate corpses will be eaten by the worm and remain in the lake of fire for all eternity. He states that they will be an abhorrence to all mankind forever. Apparently, Elohiym has purposed this as a sign to the world of His righteousness.

Notice how it said "those who *transgress*". We established very early on that there is only one thing we can transgress, and that is the Father's Torah. We have also just seen in Revelation that books will be opened to judge us by our deeds. I think we have all the evidence we need.

In the end we will all face judgment for the deeds we have committed in this life, whether good or bad. Revelation tells us this, as well as all of the Torah. Yes, this stands in incredibly stark contradiction to the theology of all modern Christian churches, but the truth is merely the truth. Scripture has exposed this to us, and not men. Scripture hasn't the ability of an ulterior motive. It needs no money, parsonage or car. It just does what it was intended to do all along…teach for free. That's why it seems so ugly and brash at times. Scripture's paycheck does not depend on tickling the ears of the masses. Scripture has no interest in not offending you or I. It wasn't created to comfort us no matter how we live, it was created to *direct* us how to live so that we might be comforted:

Jeremiah 6: [16] *Thus says YHWH:*

"Stand in the ways and see,
<u>__And ask for the ancient paths__</u>, where the good way is,
<u>__And walk in it__</u>;
Then you will find <u>__rest for your souls__</u>."

In the end, I hope that you have found truth in the many scriptures I have quoted herein. It is my sincerest desire that I have stirred something inside of you. I hope that I have driven you to dig into scripture for yourself, and see its true meaning without the slant of men who stand benefit from your attendance. If you have taken the words of Elohiym quoted within in these pages to heart, then you see there are some issues that are irreconcilable no matter *how* your pastor addresses them. Remember, his words are not more important than the word of Elohiym. If his words in any way contradict the words of the Father found in these scriptures, we must ere on the side of the word of Elohiym. The words of Elohiym are the only words that matter. This applies to me as well. Don't just take my word for it, search out all these matters for yourself.

Remember what I said in the preface, about how we don't ask enough questions? It's true. And yet another concept that is taught by scripture:

1John 4: [1]*Beloved, <u>__do not believe every spirit__</u>, but <u>__test the spirits__</u> to see whether they are from Elohiym, <u>__because many false prophets have gone out into the world__</u>.*

We absolutely *must* question everything. We must open our bibles, lexicons and concordances. We must get down to the root of the matter. Our eternity hangs in the balance. Our eternal separation from Elohiym, or glory in His presence depends upon the man behind the pulpit…*if* we have placed that trust in him. If we have, then we must test him. John clearly understood this situation, and taught that we must test to see if they are from Elohiym.

How do we know if one is against Elohiym? Torah tells us that:
"if he speaks to turn you away from the way YHWH your Elohiym commanded you to walk, then he is a false prophet" (Deut. 13:5).

What is "the way" we have all been commanded to walk? In His Torah:

Ecclesiastes 12: *13 The conclusion, when all has been heard, is: fear Elohiym and keep His commandments, because this applies to every person.*

Finally, to finish the book with the theme of two or three witnesses, a word from the Brit Chadasha and Paul about obedience to the Word:

www.ingramcontent.com/pod-product-compliance
Lightning Source LLC
Chambersburg PA
CBHW020129180726
47992CB00020B/2563